Transforming Quality Organizations

Transforming Quality Organizations

A Practical Guide

Matthew P. Wictome and Ian Wells

BUSINESS EXPERT PRESS

Leader in applied, concise business books

Transforming Quality Organizations: A Practical Guide

Copyright © Business Expert Press, LLC, 2023.

Cover design by Shutterstock / Theromb

Interior design by Exeter Premedia Services Private Ltd., Chennai, India

First published in 2023 by
Business Expert Press, LLC
222 East 46th Street, New York, NY 10017
www.businessexpertpress.com

ISBN-13: 978-1-63742-440-7 (paperback)
ISBN-13: 978-1-63742-441-4 (e-book)

Business Expert Press Supply and Operations Management Collection

First edition: 2023

10 9 8 7 6 5 4 3 2 1

All the authors' proceeds from this book will go to Patient Safety Movement, *a charity that funds research into preventable harm and death in healthcare: www.psmf.org*

Description

Is your Quality organization holding your business back? Is regulatory compliance seen as more important than product or service quality? Do you feel the needs of your customers are being lost in a sea of regulations?

Transforming Quality Organizations: A Practical Guide questions whether the current approach to managing quality is fit for purpose. It takes a fresh look at how quality can be more effectively managed and will show you practical ways to:

- Manage risk for better patient, customer, regulator, and stockholder outcomes.
- Achieve balance between ensuring compliance and supporting innovation.
- Transform your Quality organization through a roadmap of change.

Applicable to all businesses where quality is paramount, the content is based on practical experience of executing transformational change in a range of healthcare businesses resulting in the following:

- Product recalls rates cut by 50 percent.
- New product development cycle time cut by 50 percent.
- Significant cost savings in quality system execution.

This book is invaluable for business leaders who want to transform their quality organization and increase the value it delivers for your business.

Keywords

quality management; quality organizations; organizational transformation; business success; lean quality; organizational complexity; systems thinking; complexity science

Contents

Testimonials

"*This book offers a unique perspective on managing your quality system, with both strategic and practical advice for leaders who are looking to maximize their business impact.*"—**Jennifer Paine, Senior VP, Global Regulatory Affairs, Medical Devices**

"*The first quality management systems book I have read that focuses more on solving problems and achieving opportunities and provides frameworks and methodologies to achieve these goals.*"—**Thomas Stevenson, Chief Operating Officer, Medical Devices**

"*The book describes the integration of quality theory to practical application in a refreshing way, that's an excellent reference book for those driving operational transformation in their business.*"—**Ian Elliott, Retired Chief Operations Officer, Medical Devices**

"*Highlights the importance of balancing quality with healthcare compliance and shows how you can transform your quality organization and system to help your business be more effective and efficient.*"—**Àngels Roma VP QRA, In Vitro Diagnostics**

Preface

Quality of product or service is *the* critical success factor in the healthcare industry. Driven by an increasing number of healthcare issues over recent years, governments worldwide have increased their focus on regulating businesses designing, manufacturing, and distributing medical products and services. Ever more demanding regulatory requirements and standards have been issued and the enforcement powers of agencies responsible for patient safety have increased. This response is understandable but has thrown up several unique and critical dilemmas for businesses in the healthcare sector.

Whether increased regulation translates into improved patient safety is yet to be seen. It can certainly be argued that the effort and resources required to comply with increased regulation competes with those needed to understand and meet customer expectations and comes at a significant financial cost to a business.

We will argue that regulatory compliance has now become potentially confused with the concept of quality. Quality resources are, at times, seen as primarily focused on ensuring the business meets its compliance responsibilities, as opposed to improving quality. There is now a danger of organizations creating goods and services that are compliant but fall short of meeting customer needs and are potentially financially nonviable options for a business.

Secondly, control and standardization are at odds with the agile, flexible, and innovative capabilities that organizations need to meet continuously increasing customer expectations. It can be argued that compliance is now out trumping quality and innovation.

In this book, we do not argue against increased regulatory compliance. What we argue for is a renewed focus on the purpose of Quality organizations and offer some practical approaches to meet the challenges of how to comply with the regulations while ensuring customer expectations are met and businesses are financially viable.

We have based the material in the book on the application of modern management theory to the quality system; looking at the way businesses really operate and questioning not only the role of Quality organizations but also how effectively they support businesses today and in the future. It is also based on experience of applying such approaches in businesses over the past 25 years, from small to large corporations.

So, who is this book for?

1. It is for Quality professionals who want to play an active part in creating effective Quality organizations that satisfy multiple competing needs.
2. It is aimed at C-suite executives, who want their Quality organizations to do more than just meet regulatory compliance needs.
3. It is also for those in other functions to help them understand the remit of the Quality organization and its untapped potential.

In this book, we will focus on the importance of thorough problem investigation and resolution, scalable management of change, and the importance of pragmatic flexible risk management. In the context of a heavily regulated industry, we will argue that pragmatic risk management is a vital requirement and, in our opinion, the foundation of effective management of quality within all organizations.

We will also cover some modern concepts of how organizations really behave; primarily, the need for Quality professionals to be aware that they are part of a complex, ever-changing system. Secondly, they have choices about how to respond to a variety of situations and challenges. This will require them to be more flexible and become more skilled in balancing control and innovation.

We will also cover how Quality organizations will need to evolve to meet changing customer demands, organizational change, and new technology. Finally, we will cover the practical aspects of executing a transformation of a Quality organization.

This book is principally focused on the healthcare industry. However, the concepts and approaches described are *equally* applicable to any business that needs to manage quality effectively and ensure that its Quality organization is in lockstep with its business partners.

Why did we write this book?

The motivation to write this book came from seeing the same issues in multiple organizations:

- A Quality team that is viewed as too conservative/risk averse.
- Compliant records being more important than customer satisfaction.
- Quality being seen as inhibiting innovation.
- Despite multiple corrective actions, product quality often remaining unchanged.

While we would not claim that this book offers a magical solution to any of the challenges listed above, we have seen that the application of the concepts described within this book have brought about significant changes in how quality is perceived and executed within a number of businesses.

This book seeks to move the Quality organization from the execution of a quality system to a place where they are fully integrated into the business process; innovatively managing process and product quality in a complex, ever-shifting regulatory landscape.

How is the book constructed? We set out our thinking as follows:

- Understanding the concept of quality and the challenges that are typically seen in the healthcare industry.
- Recognizing that the needs of customers, regulators, and business health need to be carefully balanced.
- Arguing change and pragmatic risk management are at the heart of successfully managing a business that puts patient safety first.
- Recognizing that you cannot succeed as a Quality professional unless you appreciate that you are working with immense complexity every day.
- Understanding that the situations you face cannot be addressed with "local" solutions; you need a systems-based approach to succeed.

- Recognizing you need a Quality organization that is embedded in, not apart from, your business, with the right people, processes, and technology to win.
- Arguing that to successfully move from current to future state will take time and you will need a transformation plan to get there.

How should you read this book?

Certainly, there's nothing stopping you jumping to the end and going through some of the more practical aspects of organizational transformation. We would, however, encourage you to either read the book in chapter order or revisit some of the earlier chapters, as some of the practical approaches we explain later have important theoretical foundations.

These concepts have been applied by us at multiple organizations and are a summation of our experiences, successes, and failures. We have defined and refined our thinking about how to approach quality over many years; we will continue to do so and hope that this book provides both inspiration and guidance for you to successfully transform your own organizations.

CHAPTER 1

Quality

The Impact of Quality

Every business leader says they understand the importance of quality. It is almost a given for any member of an Executive Board to say that quality is front and center of everything they do. If asked, all will say they understand the importance and role of the quality management system (QMS).

We will argue that: (1) quality management is poorly understood within organizations, even within parts of the business tasked with managing it; (2) the role of the QMS has become misunderstood over time and has lost its original purpose; and (3) compliance has been confused with quality, and the true customers of the QMS are now largely forgotten in some organizations.

We seldom pause to reflect how the products we manufacture, especially if they are in the healthcare sector, can have a transformational impact on people's lives. Every diagnostic test, every surgical implant, every medical procedure has the potential to enhance, invigorate, or even save a life. The importance of quality obviously goes beyond these industries. No industry where products or services touch people's lives can say quality is unimportant.

As such, many companies now have a system in place to manage quality, often referred to as a QMS. Often, a certified QMS is a regulatory requirement to do business.

Given this, one would assume that virtually all industries would have an unwavering, laser-like focus on quality, especially those in healthcare? Well that simply isn't the case.

Over a 10-year period, poor-quality medical products have resulted in over 83,000 deaths and have been linked to over 1.7 million injuries [1]. This is despite these products being manufactured under stringent regulations and standards. Every year there are examples of defective products, malfunctioning implants, and incorrect diagnostic tests that were designed, built, or distributed under a compliant quality system. We will argue that the issue isn't with the quality system per se, but how it is perceived, executed, managed, and maintained. But to start with, what do we actually mean by quality?

"Quality" Versus "quality"

In this chapter, we will cover the many aspects around quality as an attribute. These encompass features from whether the product meets specifications, to how it looks and feels. The concept of quality is also relevant to organizational culture. It covers whether individuals have pride in their work, understand the impact of their actions, and their ability to proactively improve how they perform their jobs.

However, it is not always apparent what the Quality function does. Is it to ensure compliance against regulations? Prevent defects being manufactured? Improve product quality? Drive continuous improvement? Understand customer needs? The answer is often—yes—to all of these questions.

This lack of organizational definition is not only an issue around how the Quality function is perceived by business partners, but how the Quality organization sees its own role.

One general perception is that the Quality organization is solely tasked with the management of the quality system and to enforce compliance. They "police" the system. This, in turn, often attracts individuals who are more comfortable identifying problems than actually solving them. They may also see their primary purpose as ensuring compliance in a world that is black and white, as opposed to their real purpose of helping manage risk to ensure and improve quality. This brings us to what we mean by Quality versus quality.

Throughout this book, we will use the word "quality" to indicate the concept of value, and the word "Quality" to indicate the functional organization tasked with implementing, managing, and maintaining the QMS.

So, what does this mean for your business?

Do You Recognize Your Business?

It is possible to illustrate opposite ends of a culture of quality maturity spectrum with some subjective descriptions that provide a sense of what "immature" and "mature" may look or feel like:

An immature culture of quality might look like this:

- The Quality department is physically remote from the manufacturing process.
- The quality system is focused on compliance rather than quality.
- Design and development of new products is a long and arduous activity.
- Manufacturing is seen as being hindered by the quality system.
- Metrics are disconnected from customer needs.

A mature culture of quality might look like this:

- New product development is efficient, effective, and facilitated by Quality.
- Manufacturing is supported by a proactive, collaborative Quality function.
- Metrics drive action and measure your ability to meet customer expectations.
- The Quality department is aligned with the needs of all its business partners.
- Technology supports effective and efficient processes.
- There is evidence of quality in everything you do.

Does your organization fit into one of these two descriptions? Or is your organization somewhere in between, and you recognize elements from both? Wherever you are on this maturity spectrum, chances are that you want to move your organization from its current state to some improved position.

The first question is, why don't all organizations at least start this journey? The first reason is simply that organizations often do not see the benefit of the quality system to their overall business. While they may understand the compliance needs of the quality system, they do not fully appreciate the reach and influence it has.

Why?

Because, often, Quality organizations do not see it themselves.

The quality system has huge potential to improve the efficiency and effectiveness of your business, meet your customers' expectations, and position your organization ahead of its competitors. In many respects, compliance to the regulations is a by-product of an efficient and effective quality system. In essence, the quality system should be the blueprint of how you run your business.

There is also a lack of practical guidance on how to make impactful changes to the QMS. There is a plethora of publications around business improvement, primarily focused on manufacturing systems—be they lean or other methodologies—but a lack of guidance on how to apply not only these methodologies to the quality system but also improvement techniques specific to the quality system. This book hopes to address these gaps.

But to take a step back, how would you know something had the level of quality you were striving for?

What Is "Quality" and Why Does It Matter?

How quality could be defined and its importance to a broader audience was described by Garvin in 1987 in his Harvard Business Review article: *Competing on the Eight Dimensions of Quality* [2]. It is worth revisiting these eight dimensions considering organizations today, and modern customer needs. As groups, they are probably as good as any. They were defined prior to what we would recognize as modern quality standards; however, they start to dissect quality into components you can attempt to influence in practical ways.

1. **Performance:** This is generally driven by the customers' perception. Failure to deliver on performance expectations will generally result in loss of business. Note that customer's expectations can, and do, change.

2. **Conformance:** Organizations often focus on things that can be measured; goods and services that conform to well-defined specifications. These specifications should ideally be linked to performance.

3. **Features:** These define capabilities and give customers choice; doing the basics well is often more important than giving a myriad of options.

4. **Reliability:** Measures the probability that the product will perform as intended and has a strong link with our perception of quality.

5. **Durability:** How long you can use a product before it needs replacing. Current environmental expectations are that goods can be repaired rather than thrown away; however, much of the lack of durability of goods is now the result of rapid technological change.

6. **Customer Service:** Providing exemplary customer support is now a key attribute expected of all successful businesses.

7. **Looks:** We know it when we see it; that is, the product just looks well made from the packaging to the components to the marketing literature. This is key in building confidence in the product.

8. **Perceived Quality:** Perception is reality, and if products are perceived to be of poor quality, then the impact is the same as if they genuinely are.

Taking all these components together, we can see that quality is a multifaceted concept when viewed through the eyes of the customer. It has aspects often overlooked by organizations. The question for Quality organizations is: are you equally focused on *all* the dimensions of quality? Or do you focus on aspects that are easier to measure or those traditionally viewed as being within the jurisdiction of the Quality organization such as specifications and tolerances?

More fundamentally, does it even matter to you and your business?

Does Quality Really Matter Anymore to Businesses?

If you look at the websites of the top 10 medical device companies selling products and services intrinsically connected to patient health and safety, approximately half have no explicit mention of the importance of product quality. The remaining have a collection of generic statements buried in text extolling the virtues and importance of quality.

Poor quality costs the industry around $5 billion per year. A significant recall can cost as much as $600M [3]. It has been calculated that a company moving from average to good quality can increase its revenue by four percent [3]. So, from a financial perspective, addressing poor quality is a no-brainer.

So why is there an apparent lack of commitment to quality being shown by many big healthcare companies? Is it the case that quality is now believed to be hardwired into the DNA of the organization? Or that quality has taken a backseat to the more fashionable aspects such as sustainability, protection of the environment, diversity, and more general corporate social responsibility?

If you look at the makeup of the Executive Boards of these top 10 companies, half do not have an executive director on the board specifically responsible for quality. All healthcare companies are legally required to have a responsible person directly accountable for quality, but whether this elevates them to the executive level is not always guaranteed.

The Cost of Quality

Poor quality directly impacts your ability to deliver to the customer. Quality should reach every part of your business and influence its ability to meet customer needs and ultimately guarantee the future of your company. It doesn't matter if your goods are the cheapest on a well-stocked shelf if nobody will buy them.

But these challenges are not new. Garvin's eight dimensions of quality are no less applicable today than they were over 30 years ago. In addition, the role of quality influencing other indicators of business success isn't a new idea. It has foundations going back to the origins of quality management.

So why is a focus on quality a greater challenge today and its emphasis more pressing now than ever? The reason is twofold.

First, the impact of increasing regulations and adherence to standards today is convincing businesses that they have got quality covered, solely by compliance with regulations and standards.

Second, there is a potential conflict between 1) the systems in place to ensure control and compliance and 2) innovation and more fluid approaches needed by businesses to understand and meet current and future customer expectations.

Quality Management Systems: The Focus on Control

Medical devices constitute everything from diagnostic assays to surgical instruments to pacemakers. The safety of these devices is paramount, and in 1996, ISO13485 was introduced detailing the quality system requirements for manufacturers and distributors of medical devices [4]. Despite this, the industries that are covered by the requirements of ISO13485 have had a number of very high profile safety issues that give insight into whether standards are meeting their intent that is, improving quality.

In 2010, a French medical device company—Poly Implant Prothese— was found guilty of using low-grade silicon filler, intended to produce furniture, in the manufacture of breast implants. As a result of the use of this substandard material, one person died and over 300,000 patients required removal of the implants due to its implication with an increased risk in developing cancer. This criminal act resulted in the company going into a liquidation and several directors of the company convicted and eventually being sent to jail [5].

While standardization of quality system requirements is obviously a good thing and certainly not all companies that are certified have critical quality issues, this example demonstrates that having a recognized QMS does not always guarantee products that are safe [6, 7].

In the United States, the Food and Drug Administration's medical device quality regulations are broadly aligned with the ISO13485 standard and in many respects are even more stringent and robustly enforced [8]. Generally, the number of product recalls in the United States has been running in the region of 3,000 per year [9]. In some respects recalls are a good thing, as they protect customers from potentially unsafe products.

While recalls are a reflection that the quality system is working and companies are willing to take action to protect customers, this comes at a financial cost. It has been calculated that a single recall can result in a 10 percent drop in a company's share prices [3].

Despite this financial impact and driven by their primary purpose to protect the customer the design and manufacture of medical devices has come under increased scrutiny by regulators. Subsequently, there was further tightening of the laws around the manufacturing of such products. In 2021, in the European Union, the Medical Device Regulations came into force and brought a new level of compliance requirements around how devices are designed, manufactured, and sold.

If we return to Garvin's eight dimensions of quality, and consider the requirements of ISO13485, certain aspects stand out. The standard has a heavy focus on ensuring that the product is manufactured in compliance with processes that are in control and consistent over time. Of the eight dimensions, only three have strong basis in the standard, namely: conformance, reliability, and performance. Two have a moderate link: service and features. For the final three, the link is relatively weak: looks, perceived quality, and durability.

While it could be argued that the ISO standard covers all these aspects to a greater or lesser extent around requirements as to how products are designed, the general focus on conformance, reliability, and performance means other aspects of quality are not always considered so important. Again, even the strong focus on these three attributes themselves hasn't prevented recalls or always ensured products are made that are safe.

We would argue that compliance standards are important and drive consistency. They are generally a core requirement for manufacturing healthcare products, but do not always take a holistic approach to quality. With respect to the power of these standards, it can even be argued that their implementation can result in a mirage of improved quality. There is a sound argument that supports that compliance has become confused with quality, and this is the basis of much of the issues seen in recent years related to product safety. This aside, we argue that the standards need to be supplemented by more inclusive approaches to quality, and Quality organizations need to be transformed to meet this need.

In addition, there is another aspect of the current business climate that makes the need to transform Quality organizations more pressing: the growing conflict between increased control through regulation and the need for organizations to innovate.

Control Versus Innovation

In recent years, we have taken a more proactive role in our own health-care and there has been an explosion in the expectation that the health-care industry will give us personalized products. This has driven a huge amount of innovation. The challenge is fostering an environment of responsive innovation that supports rapid change. This is somewhat diametrically at odds with the control required by standards and regulations.

There are those who would say that there are already structured approaches to continuous improvement, such as Six Sigma and lean, that would meet the needs of managing change in more controlled regulatory environments. It is also fair to say that the application of Six Sigma and lean within the medical devices industry has been historically low, 20 and 30 percent respectively, compared with other industries such as automotive and information services [10]. In addition, the application of such approaches to quality systems is a rarity and often seen as outside of the scope of such methodology (see Figure 1.1).

Quality organizations need to take a more holistic approach to quality and compliance, and to address the need to be agile and innovative in

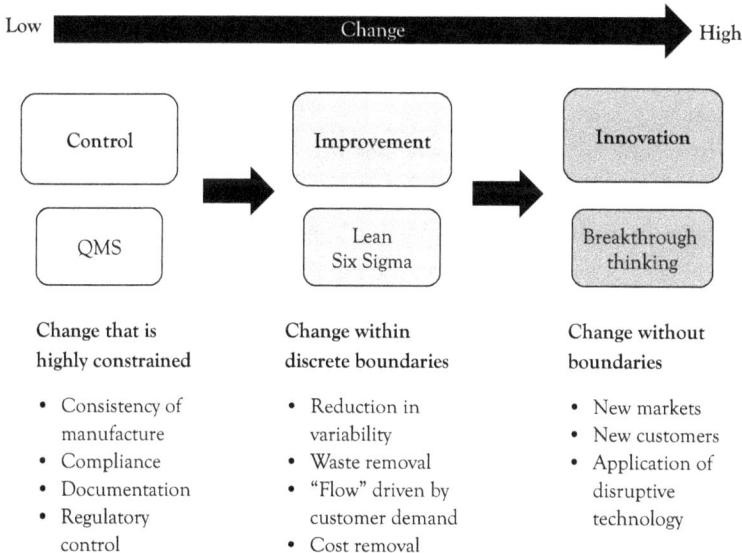

Low ———————— Change ————————→ High		
Control	**Improvement**	**Innovation**
QMS	Lean Six Sigma	Breakthrough thinking
Change that is highly constrained	Change within discrete boundaries	Change without boundaries
• Consistency of manufacture • Compliance • Documentation • Regulatory control	• Reduction in variability • Waste removal • "Flow" driven by customer demand • Cost removal	• New markets • New customers • Application of disruptive technology

Figure 1.1 Control versus innovation

meeting increasing customer demands. It requires a transformation over how Quality organizations are viewed, operate, and behave. Certainly, it requires organizations to define where they are and develop a strategy to transform how the Quality function behaves and is viewed by others.

Building a Quality Strategy

Before developing a quality strategy, it is worth exploring beliefs around quality. These can be organizational and personal. Is quality an important aspect that you as a leader think is critical to your business's success? What are your organizational beliefs around this attribute? Do all parts of the organization have a true understanding of what quality is, why it is important, and how this translates into behaviors in the workplace?

In trying to get answers to the question of an individual's approach to quality, there is one huge barrier. Shocking as it may seem, sometimes people, and organizations, don't always say what they truly mean.

Like all views, we have a personal view, one we may or may not keep to ourselves, and an external view that we project. This may be the same as our internal view, or it may be different due to a myriad of reasons. These include the need to project your organization's values and belief systems, as a way of fitting in, or it is simply the way you behave in an organization, that is, saying what you think the organization wants to hear.

This book isn't to judge whether this is right or wrong. It is just the way people and organizations behave. Figure 1.2 illustrates the two opposites of quality and its internal/external perspective and shows how individuals perceive quality from the public and personal point of view.

The bottom left-hand quadrant describes organizations and people who have a low opinion of the importance of quality, and frankly are not concerned how this view comes across. These are the cowboy/rogue traders of the world who (generally) do not last.

The bottom right-hand quadrant covers those who work in organizations not renowned for a commitment to quality, but they are the pockets of excellence who take pride in their work, despite all around them having a different view.

Opposing Views on Quality

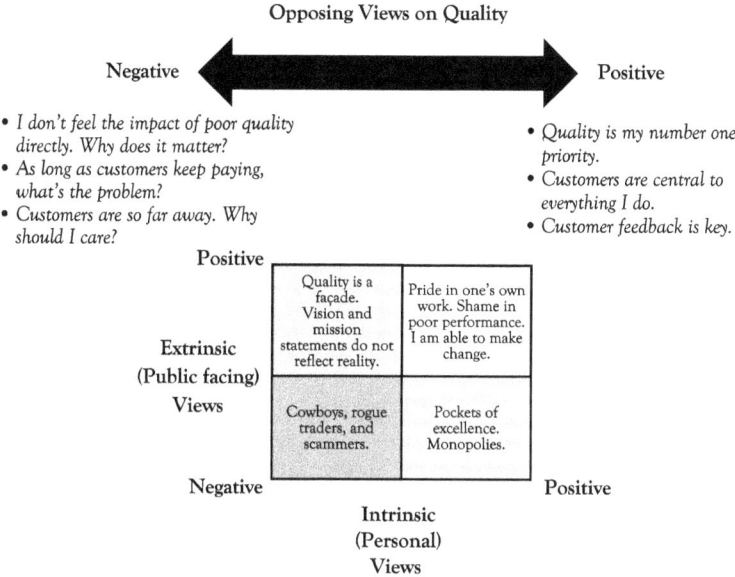

Negative ◄━━━━━━━━━━━━━━► Positive

- *I don't feel the impact of poor quality directly. Why does it matter?*
- *As long as customers keep paying, what's the problem?*
- *Customers are so far away. Why should I care?*

- *Quality is my number one priority.*
- *Customers are central to everything I do.*
- *Customer feedback is key.*

Positive

	Quality is a façade. Vision and mission statements do not reflect reality.	Pride in one's own work. Shame in poor performance. I am able to make change.
Extrinsic (Public facing) Views		
	Cowboys, rogue traders, and scammers.	Pockets of excellence. Monopolies.

Negative   Positive

Intrinsic
(Personal)
Views

Figure 1.2 Quality views and external/internal perspective

The top left quadrant is probably where a lot of organizations sit. These are businesses and individuals where the importance of quality is trumpeted. This, however, does not translate into true understanding and commitment. To maintain organizations in this group takes a huge amount of management energy and resources, as the messaging must be constantly reinforced across the business and practice policed.

The top right quadrant is where we'd like all businesses to be. The value of quality is understood by everyone and demonstrated in the products and services it offers. There is pride in the work people do, and this translates into a customer experience that is valued and recognized. In addition, individuals feel part of the organization and empowered to make improvements to the way the customer is served.

These four quadrants are not mutually exclusive. It is possible to have individuals even in the same department with each of the four different perspectives. As a leader, you have huge power to influence this positioning. Though it may not be possible to always move everybody and the organization completely into the top right quadrant, the closer you are, the better it will be for your business.

Building a Strategy

Any strategy will be based on where you want to get to, and how far you feel your organization is from being in the place you want it to be. This roadmap to the future will obviously be influenced by the current state of your organization. It will require a degree of honest benchmarking of where you are. The road map can be broken down into three components: People, Process, and Technology.

You will need to consider all these aspects and the following chapters will help you define where you are, where you want to be, and how to get there. As we will cover, transforming a Quality organization is more than implementing the latest shiny application and cloud-based platform. It is about integrating all the above aspects together. One aspect that is key is how you approach strategy.

Planned, Emergent, or Zero Strategy

There are scores of business books on strategy, and this essentially boils down to either having a fixed strategy, no strategy at all, or something in between.

At one extreme, planned strategy involves a defined and well-laid-out plan of how you are going to get where you want to go. It will have milestones, tasks, and who is responsible for delivering them. The drawback with a planned strategy is that the real world gets in the way. Events occur, technology moves on, and priorities and customer needs change.

At the other end of the spectrum is having no strategy at all, essentially making it up as you go along and reacting to events as they happen. However, events will shape your business and the wind of change will blow you in any direction it wants. You will become a business follower rather than a business leader.

Emergent strategy is in between. You have a strategy based on what you know at the time. You assess risk and attempt to predict what you can but accept that the plan will always need a degree of course correction along the way. Such an approach will require you to behave differently.

You will need to look for patterns in data and information and be able to exploit changes. Here, strategy should be seen not as a noun, but as a verb and an activity that is ongoing rather than a onetime event. Such an approach will need you to see organizations not as machines that are always highly predictable, but systems that require a more fluid approach to strategy. In practice, the most effective approach to strategy is to set out with a plan but actively modify it as you need to.

Summary

Don't confuse quality with compliance. Compliance is about showing you are meeting your regulatory requirements. Quality is demonstrating you are meeting your customer needs.

- Whether you are selling a product or service—quality impacts all aspects of your business, from cost, patient safety, and compliance to your customers' experience. It is crucial that it gets your leadership attention.
- Focusing on quality from a purely regulatory or compliance perspective won't prevent your next costly recall. You need to look at quality in a holistic way.
- You need your quality system to be able to balance control (compliance) with agility (innovation) to be successful.

You will need an agile quality strategy to detail how you will improve, grow, and protect your business going forward.

CHAPTER 2

Balancing the QMS

This chapter frames what the concept of "customer" means for quality management and attempts to address some of the disconnects that have arisen over recent years regarding customer focus. It will reexamine some of the customer-focused methodology and how it can be applied within the context of the QMS. It also attempts to explain how the role of the customer can simultaneously act as a reference point to determine whether your QMS is effective in meeting customer needs, and also how the concept of customer needs can sometimes distract you from meeting their expectations.

Customers Have Choice

Customers know what is important to them and what isn't. They don't care where your distribution centers are; how easy or hard it is for you to manufacture your products; whether your QMS is paper based or electronic or even whether you have standardized your inventory systems across your plants. Yet these are the types of projects many Quality units are involved with. The one thing customers care a lot about and take very seriously is, quality. Customers have the power to say "No." They can refuse to pay for goods or services received or choose to use another supplier in the future, and they have a unique relationship with you in that:

1. Their relationship is never subordinate to you.
2. The customer can take their business elsewhere if needed.

Customers generally hold all the power in the relationship with you.

The Myth That Is the "Internal Customer"

Over the past 20 years there has been a growing concept that, within organizations, there are internal customers. For example, the warehouse is viewed as a customer of the packing line. The concept of internal customers within organizations is a relatively new one. Peter Drucker—one of the pioneers of quality management—was less supportive of this idea and his view was that the only customer that existed was the external customer who paid the bills [11].

So, are internal customers true "customers" in the traditional sense? No, they are not. They do not meet the two criteria of the customer/supplier relationship.

Is the external customer the only one who meets the true definition of a customer, when we talk about quality? Well, no. Other customers exist.

Who Are the Customers of the Quality System?

The QMS exists to ensure that customers receive a product that is safe, reliable, and meets all their expectations. As such, the external customer is obviously the primary customer of the quality system. There may be layers of external customer. For example, the distributor of the product (e.g., a diagnostic test) and the testing laboratory that uses the diagnostic product or the patient whose blood is tested are all layers of external customers. These customers have the power to stop buying from your business and purchase from another organization whose quality system is better able to serve their needs. Note that the customer has little interest in the mechanics of your QMS, only that the output gives them what they want.

But the quality system goes beyond just satisfying the customer. Many industries require that the QMS be assessed at intervals and meet the relevant regulations or standards. Customers generally care little about this, but regulatory bodies take a great interest in the mechanics of how you are meeting these requirements. They also have the power as a true customer to say no. In extreme cases they can prevent you from selling or distributing your goods.

Because of the amount of power a regulatory agency wields, the misconception sometimes felt throughout the business is that the QMS exists purely to satisfy the regulators and the sole purpose of the Quality function is to operate the QMS to meet this end.

But there is also another voice at the table. Businesses need to make a profit, be economically and environmentally sustainable, have funds to reinvest in new products and facilities, and pay shareholders their dividend. Organizations may have the best quality products in the customers' eyes with a QMS that is highly compliant but if the business is not making a profit, it will not survive. Business health is also a key customer of the QMS.

So, in summary there are three customers of the QMS:

- Customer Experience
- Regulatory Compliance
- Business Health

As we shall explain, each customer may have different views on what is important.

Concept of Value and the Role of Perspective

In process improvement terminology, value has a very specific meaning related to how the product is changed and whether the customer would be willing to pay for this change. It involves concepts such as "value added" and "nonvalue added" time and "mapping the value stream." Here the concept of value will be restricted to the traditional definition of value as being something that a customer considers important.

Different customers will consider different aspects of the QMS more important than others. As a leader you will try to balance the needs of all the customers and identify win:wins such that everybody gets what they want.

Customer Experience

The customer is primarily concerned about three aspects of the goods or services that you provide: (1) safety and quality, (2) availability, and (3) price.

Generally, the customer will accept a trade-off regarding one aspect against another, but unless you have a monopoly or can differentiate your products in the market, you will have to satisfy these three criteria to retain current and secure new customers. The quality system, though focused primarily on quality will also impact to a greater or lesser extent your ability to meet these three requirements.

Compliance

The regulatory bodies who assess compliance against quality system standards have a different vantage point with respect to how they view your QMS. They are concerned that you can demonstrate, with objective evidence, that you are meeting the requirements of the appropriate standard or regulation. While customer satisfaction is incorporated in several quality standards such as the ISO9001 series, the content of many standards is often primarily focused on ensuring the product is safe and consistently manufactured.

Examples of data that they would use as evidence their expectations were being met include evidence of management of product or process changes, control of measuring and test equipment, document management, design controls, and data-driven decision making.

For your regulatory agencies to be satisfied they must look at aspects of your QMS and find convincing evidence demonstrating that these requirements are being satisfied. Owing to this focus, it is possible to have metrics that measure compliance but not a strong link with product performance and therefore final customer satisfaction. Examples include:

1. The average time to close a complaint.
2. The number of staff without approved training plans.
3. The number of corrective and preventive action (CAPA) events open in the quality system.
4. The number of open service orders with customers.

It is a common mistake during quality system management review (QSMR) that such metrics are confused with the output of the quality system, but they are simply measures of the QMS operating. Often, they are presented as key performance indicators (KPIs) but are neither key nor true indicators of performance of the system. Taking the previous examples, better customer focused metrics would be as follows:

1. The percentage of complaints closed to the customer's satisfaction.
2. The number of deviations in manufacturing because of inadequate training.
3. The number of ineffective CAPA events implemented.
4. The percentage of customers with equipment that cannot be used due to reliability issues.

How many of the metrics you measure within your QMS are focused on the customer? How many charts do you review that give just the illusion of performance?

Aside from this aspect of QMS metrics measuring activity and not system output, the harsh reality is that all businesses requiring a certifiable quality system need to demonstrate that they comply to stay in business. To this end, it does require a degree of activity to demonstrate that you are meeting the expectations of the relevant standard and are compliant. However, a system that is compliant does not always equate to one that is good.

Business Health

When the QMS is discussed in a business context, it is invariably seen through the lens of cost. In the case of highly regulated industries, these activities are often viewed as costs that must be tolerated in order for the business to trade. This is a narrow and one-dimensional view of the quality system: the QMS has a huge role to play in ensuring that the business is healthy and sustainable.

The three customers of the QMS all have a key attribute of a true customer, that is, they have the power of choice. Regulatory bodies can refuse to approve your QMS; your customers can take their business elsewhere and your shareholders can decide not to invest in your business.

Investing in the quality system should be seen in the same light as investing in new products, markets, and technologies. All investments require costs to be incurred but underinvesting in quality can come at a far greater cost to the business, either financially or reputationally.

Different Customers, Different Perspectives

An effective QMS needs to balance the needs of these three groups and different functions in an organization will generally have more focus on one customer aspect than another.

The quality assurance manager would be rightly concerned that defective material was securely bonded and wasn't shipped. While his peer, the manufacturing manager would be more concerned about whether this material would be released or lost to scrap. This differing perception of value is very important as it helps define measures over what is important to the customer (see Table 2.1).

It is possible by systematically moving through each section of the QMS and putting on a series of hats (metaphorically speaking) to define metrics, which give a better measure of true quality system performance, ones that the customer considers valuable.

Table 2.1 Different perspectives on the same QMS subsystem—control of nonconforming product—and its respective performance measurement

Customer	Perspective	Performance Measurement
Compliance (QA)	"I need to ensure that non-conforming product is bonded, secure and will not be released"	The number of nonconformances related to inappropriate release of bonded product.
Business Health (Manufacturing)	"If the nonconforming is to be scrapped or released back into inventory, I need this decision quickly"	Cycle-time to release or scrap nonconforming product.

Balancing the QMS

As the adage goes "you can please some of the people all of the time, you can please all of the people some of the time, but you can't please all of the people all of the time"—but as a leader with responsibilities for the performance of the quality system that is what you will need to do. Obviously, some areas push in the same direction. For example, giving your customers products that meet their expectations should help the bottom line. However, there are times when the three customers of the QMS may be pulling in different directions. The QMS, though compliant, may become overly bureaucratic and those responsible for it miss the point of why it exists. Conversely, the race to supply products and keep the shelves stocked may result in cutting corners and lead to significant regulatory and patient risk.

So how can you satisfy customers of the quality system who often have competing and conflicting expectations? No book can give you these answers but there is one approach that should be the first port of call for any attempt to manage a customer-centric QMS: Simplification.

In general, the more you can simplify aspects of the QMS the more you will be able to meet the different needs of its three customers. Processes that are simple are generally better able to react to customer needs, are less prone to error, are less costly to build and maintain, and are generally easier to comply with.

However, if only it were so simple. As we will cover in later chapters, attempts to impose complete control, and standardize the quality system will usually fail due to specific aspects of how the quality system operates as a complex system. The imposition of control has diminishing returns and will eventually stifle innovation and agility. How the quality system can be positioned optimally—between complete control and complete freedom—will be covered later, but first we will review some examples of simplification of the quality system (using standard manufacturing/ process improvement methodologies) that can help the end customer, regulatory position, and your business health.

Doing the Basics

Gaining Control

If your QMS is in a state of chaos: if documents are regularly lost or maybe never created, if basic good manufacturing practice (GMP) is not being followed and practices that border on the illegal are being tolerated, then you need to gain control immediately.

How you address this will send a strong signal on your commitment and hugely impact the success with which you are able to make further changes down the line. As the saying goes—you get what you tolerate—and the QMS is no different.

Completing an Inventory

You'll need to complete an inventory of what you have in your QMS. You will also need to create a current state map. As we will return to later, it is useful in considering current state to split the quality system into the following categories: People, Processes, and Technology. Start by reviewing your procedures, while probably the driest form of understanding the QMS it is the same approach that an auditor would use to assess the suitability of your QMS. Then carry out interviews, horizontally and vertically throughout the organization. Include key stakeholder functions. Ask how do individuals feel about the importance of quality and their perception of the quality system? One of the issues as a leader is people often tell you what they think you want to hear, and not the truth. Consider surveys that allow anonymity to get more honest feedback. Then assess your QMS for People, Processes, and Technology:

- People
  - o Does everybody have an attitude toward quality that you feel is appropriate?
  - o What is the organizational structure within Quality and the interfaces between other functions?
  - o Do you have the correct skills and competencies now and for the future?
  - o What is the staff turnover and how is succession planned?
  - o Who are the movers and shakers within your organization?
- Processes
  - o What does your process map look like?
  - o Are the quality management processes efficient, effective, and meeting customer needs?
  - o Is Quality linked to other functions, at both the strategic and tactical level?

o How much is the QMS paper based versus electronic?

o How do you manage the significant systems within the QMS?

o What is the governance model for the QMS?

- Technology

  o Is technology helping your people do their jobs more easily and more effectively?

  o Where are the data silos and how are they managed?

  o How much is automated versus manual?

Once you have completed the above exercise you should have a good idea of where the Quality organization is positioned and how the concept of quality and the QMS is viewed, executed, and maintained. Now you can start about making some basic improvements.

Spring Cleaning

You need to decide what you want to keep, what needs to go into the waste skip and generally laying the ground for any more changes you want to make. We recommend the lean methodology, 5S, be applied to the QMS for this goal.

The advantage of following this methodology is that it does give structure to the approach. The 5S approach—like all tools—needs to be used with a large dose of common sense. Sadly, it is possible to apply the methodology too religiously and go overboard. Watch out also, as the process needs to be applied once you have the system under a degree of control, or it may standardize a system that is out of kilter. The next section gives the five stages (Sort, Set, Shine, Standardize, Sustain) of the methodology and more specifically how it can be applied to aspects of the quality system.

Sort: The process starts with working out what you need. If you don't use something, throw it away or store it until you require it. Things to consider include: Can procedures, documents, and forms be obsoleted? Do you really need them? Are there forms of uncontrolled documents in the workplace, such as reminders and cheat-sheets?

Set in order: This step involves making sure you have things close to where they are needed. Are procedures and instructions for executing the QMS readily available at point of use? Does Quality have ready access to the data they need to make the appropriate decisions?

Shine: Is the work area clean and presentable? Are records sorted and stored systematically? Remove uncontrolled notes/documents from GMP areas.

Standardize: Consider using visuals, that is, graphics and flowcharts within procedures to explain the stages of the process. Add checklists to error proof that the key stages have been carried out in the necessary order. Use visual indicators so that you know when things aren't correct, and the workplace is drifting away from where you want it to be.

Sustain: The final step is focused on ensuring that the gains made during the previous stages are maintained. In terms of the QMS, conduct (1) regular audits to check that systems have been maintained, and (2) periodic review of documents to ensure that they reflect what is executed, and that they are up to date and consistent with both internal documents and external standards and regulations.

Following these steps will help start laying the foundations for some of the improvements to come, during your QMS transformation. The next stage is looking at the QMS to help visualize some of the different types of waste in the system getting in the way of its ability to satisfy its customers.

Removing Waste

Waste gets in the way of fulfilling customer needs. This is one of the foundations of lean manufacturing. The same applies to waste within the QMS. Waste can take on many guises and is often less apparent and hidden, though no less impactful compared with waste within the production system. The next section covers the standard eight types of waste often categorized and how they translate with specific examples in the context of the quality system. Waste removal is one of the foundations for creating a more efficient and effective QMS.

There are two areas where the QMS is involved in the generation of waste. First, waste creation within the areas it supports, for example: Customer Experience, Business Health, and Compliance. Secondly as a business system itself. The QMS has waste within its own transactional processes. We describe the eight types of waste in the following.

Waste 1: Defects

Defects within the QMS include validation deviations, nonconformances for not following procedures, incorrect supplier specifications, inaccurate technical reports, corrupt quality data, and misaligned quality objectives and key performance indicators.

Methods for addressing root cause will be covered in the next chapter, but suitable approaches for reducing defects in the quality system include meaningful specifications, standard work, error proofing, Six Sigma approaches to reduce variability, clear procedures, data verification, improved QSMR, and rigorous application of the CAPA system.

Waste 2: Inventory

Excessive inventory is a waste as it involves keeping items that are not needed. Types of inventories related to the quality system include excessive number of documents that are required to be periodically reviewed, irrelevant information being collected, quality data that is collected but never reviewed, and quality records that are no longer needed.

Ways of addressing excessive inventory within the QMS include reducing the number of controlled documents, remove all nonrelevant information from procedures, prune back, question whether all specifications are needed and are critical to quality or function, remove any requirement to capture irrelevant data.

Waste 3: Waiting

This waste includes waiting for (1) approval of documents, (2) approval of batch records for product release, (3) point resource to become available, (4) test results, and (5) management approval and waiting for critical meetings to take place. Much of the waiting in the QMS is waiting for information or approval of information.

Ways of reducing waiting include eliminating sequential document approvals (bring approvers together to execute the review/approval as a group), cross training to eliminate point resource, ensuring approvals are always able to be delegated with documented accountability, reducing the number of approvals on documents, driving accountability for document approval down to the lowest management level possible.

Waste 4: Overproduction

Overproduction includes excessive documentation that goes beyond requirements, multiple copies of documents, and excessive data that is not required.

Much of the over production in the QMS is documentation that is just not needed and only gives an illusion of compliance and control. Ways of reducing over production include ensuring that documents do not go beyond what is required, utilizing electronic workflows to remove multiple redundant paper copies of documents, and collecting only data that is necessary.

Waste 5: Motion

Waste from excessive movement of people or equipment includes searching for documentation, moving data from one software application to another, trying to find the correct individual to approve a report, walking to the printer/scanner, and so on.

Much of the motion in the QMS is where information or materials are not close to where they are needed. Ways of reducing excessive motion include using electronic systems that allow documentation to be available at point of need and allow approvals within a workflow from any location.

Waste 6: Overprocessing

Waste from performing activities that go beyond what the customer requires. For example: collecting data that is not needed, duplication of data entry, specifications that are not necessary or are narrower than required, and redundant or duplicate release testing.

Ways to address overprocessing include reviewing specifications to determine whether these are needed or too narrow, only collecting data that is needed, moving incoming inspection activities to the supplier and removing unnecessary testing.

Waste 7: Transport

Waste from excessive transportation of materials or products. For example, moving the physical batch record around with the product, moving reports between departments for signatures, and moving data between individuals and systems.

Ways of addressing excessive transportation include moving the QMS closer to production, replacing paper batch records with electronic batch records, having central databases that can be accessed remotely, and connecting databases together.

Waste 8: Talent

Waste from not utilizing talent, skills, and experience. Ways to address wasted talent include developing a thorough Training and Development program, cross training, recognizing and celebrating high achievement, carrying out a skills audit and understanding your inventory of talent, using the creative power of employees and building diversity of views, skills, and opinions.

Summary

You will need to build a balanced QMS.

- Your quality system has many customers with equally valid needs.
- You need to look at the quality system and ask is it satisfying all these needs?
- Do not reinvent the wheel. Apply proven service and manufacturing improvement approaches to the quality system to simplify and remove waste.
- You need to focus on outcomes of the quality system rather than its activity.

CHAPTER 3

Change

It's a Messy, Messy World

This book takes a slightly different approach to other business books on change. Most texts take the view that businesses that proactively manage change, become agile and can seize the opportunities will be the winners. By applying appropriate methods, rigorously and consistently, your business will eventually be in control. However, even after the application of such approaches over the past 50 years or more—this is simply not true for many organizations.

Driving change is usually seen as a proactive and positive activity. This is not always correct. Any change has the potential to create good or bad outcomes and is highly dependent on the perspectives of those that take part in the process. In addition, despite the aspirations of leaders to proactively manage events and make their businesses better, most issues that business leaders deal with on a day-to-day basis are simply reacting to the stuff of business. We challenge any leader to say that they are dealing with less issues today, than they were 20 years ago. True, the topics may be different, but the challenges remain the same.

Leaders often argue that if only they could get through those specific set of events, have the latest cloud-based application, put in place a better business structure, and so on, they could get to a little island of stability where they could more proactively manage their business.

History tells us this will not happen.

So, why does this matter?

It matters because we often accept less rigorous approaches as we muddle through scenarios; we do not probe issues as deeply as we should and often put in place weaker solutions, as we treat the current issue as the exception rather than the rule. Moving and fluctuating events squeeze our ability to be as exacting as we would like or should be.

This matters because change is never driven from a position of having enough time, resources, and intellectual space to make considered decisions. Most change models operate in an ideal environment, never in the reality of a messy, changing, and conflicting world.

Despite whatever the change models say—change is not always urgent. Many frameworks talk about creating a sense of urgency, articulating the burning platform or the golden opportunity that will be lost if we do not act with expediency. Certain changes, though not urgent, are just important and need to happen. Certain changes may have long lead times or are needed to prepare the ground for other changes. As you will see, this is a key component in the transformational map that you will need to build to plan, prioritize, and communicate the quality system transformation you want to make.

The final difference in our approach relates more to boundaries of the change process. Change management is generally focused on how change is implemented and made effective. The bookshelves are full of texts detailing how to best manage change in organizations, with the latest frameworks and models to follow. These frameworks often fail because they are so focused on the management of change as opposed to asking two highly pertinent questions.

1. Is the problem I am trying to address the correct one?
2. Is the solution I am putting in place the most appropriate?

Most change textbooks get lost in the management of the change that these two key questions are sometimes forgotten. For this reason, this chapter is called "Change" as opposed to "Management of Change" and will cover key practical aspects such as identifying problems and finding the best solutions. This is important as often when the change management ship has set sail, it is impossible to bring it back into the harbor and you are left implementing a poor solution for the wrong problem.

Change Management in the Context of the QMS

One would expect clear direction as to how change should be managed within the standards that define QMSs. Sadly, this is not always the case. In the 9001 series of standards this aspect is covered in various parts detailing how changes to the quality system should be planned, controlled, and managed.

Similarly, the standard covering medical devices (ISO13485) articulates the need to assess the impact of any change on the performance of the device and similarly any impact on the QMS. Neither standard has sections explicitly covering the expectations of *how* change should be managed. ISO13485 has a section specifically dedicated to how documents are controlled but none cover how change is identified, implemented, and maintained per se. This has resulted in some confusion within organizations, as it is often seen solely as a document management issue and this is often how change management is presented during an inspection that is, how documents are stored, accessed, and updated.

This understates the importance of how change should be managed and the importance of a holistic approach involving not only changes to procedures that drive actions in a risk-based manner—Change Control—but also changes to cultures and behaviors that are a key part of any impactful and sustainable change to the QMS—Change Management.

The truth is no change that really transforms a quality system or moves it forward substantially ever simply involved just changing a document or procedure.

With respect to the reasons for making changes, change may be instigated by a number of factors originating from the three customer groups described previously.

Under Customer Experience, change may be to improve the customer experience of the product, with respect to performance and reliability. Change may be driven by technological improvements to reduce risks associated with the manufacturing process. Change may also be the result of new customer requirements.

Under Compliance, change may be due to the need to meet the requirements of current or updated regulations or standards that could impact either process and/or product. Perversely, compliance is often used as a reason not to change.

Under Business Health, change may be the result of the need to improve the efficiency of the business to ensure its viability and the ability to reinvest resources to drive business growth and support existing or new markets.

All of these are valid reasons for making changes to the quality system that are linked to improving aspects its customers view as important. Sadly, there are often many times change happens that has no link to customer need and just gives the illusion of benefit.

So, if you have decided making a change to the QMS is in its customers' best interest, what is the best process to follow?

Traditional Change Management Models

Generally, all change models involve making the organization receptive for change, transitioning the change, and then locking the change into the business. The benefit of following a change model is that you are essentially coloring by numbers and even the most amateur painter can drive and implement a change initiative by following several logical steps. The prime deficiency in change models is that the world is not as logical and ordered as we would like it to be. In 1995, Kotter proposed an eight-stage model of how change could be implemented in organizations and forms the basis of many other change frameworks [12].

Kotter's Change Model

1. *Create a Sense of Urgency*

   However, not all change is urgent, but many changes are important. Creating an environment where everything is urgent can create an environment where nothing is urgent. Urgency offers up a challenge between differentiating what needs doing as part of the day job and what should be done as part of the change, which one should take priority?

   In summary, be wary of articulating that everything is urgent. It is not, but your job as a leader is to decide what is important and what must change.

2. *Build a Guiding Team*

   Change cannot be delivered without the visible support of the senior leadership team. One reason that change initiatives fail is due to a lack of management support or support that is only superficial. It is key that you directly involve those impacted by the change in the change exercise itself, both to ensure that the end customers' needs are considered and the voice of the customer, either internally or externally, is heard.

Members of the guiding team may also have vested interests and often personal political capital invested in the effort. Your role as leader is to be cognizant of this and take a big-picture view of the direction you want your organization to head in.

3. *Develop the Vision*

If you are a leader tasked to transform a Quality organization, then essentially the challenge to deliver a better future for customer, regulatory and business health is yours. Own it, develop it, and nurture it. Certainly, seek diverse views to get better perspectives to make better decisions, but at the end of the day the vision is yours.

If we pause and review the first three steps of Kotter's model, first it is difficult to understand how a sense of urgency can be instilled prior to building a coalition and developing a vision for change. We would argue that these three steps happen simultaneously.

Organizations want to understand where they are going and the means to getting there. Individuals are often more concerned with how the change will impact them directly. Even if the change may impact them negatively, most people would rather know. There should be a large degree of transparency in the change process. In the absence of clear, credible explanations, individuals will see hidden agendas or build worst case scenarios which will disrupt you.

If you are transforming a Quality organization, then you are doing it to improve the business, customer experience and to make individual's jobs easier for them to perform. Repeat this message as often and as clearly as you can. What is the problem you are trying to solve, what is the best solution and what is the journey to implementing this solution? In essence, you will need a transformation map to articulate the voyage ahead.

In our experience, the transformation map—or T-Map—is the optimum tool to describe the strategic journey of an organization (of any size) from current to desired future state over a medium-term time frame (typically 3–5 years). We will describe how to build a T-Map and its use as part of a strategic transformation in Chapter 8.

4. *Communicate for Buy-In*

One of the other reasons that change programs fail is through poor communication. The T-map described previously will help communicate your plan. The plan must be seen to be credible and not a flash in the pan or the latest fad being rolled out. Be careful with branding any initiative that could give the impression of style over substance. The key is building credibility with a clear and consistent message. Most importantly ask yourself before communicating: what is the message I am trying to get across and what do I want my audience to do differently as a result of my message?

5. *Empower Action*

Kotter's fifth stage involves empowering action to be taken. This is easier said than done, because many leaders want to stay in control. Empowering by its very definition involves letting go and allowing individuals and groups to take control of identifying change and making change work for them. It also means allowing them to make mistakes. Your job is to help them learn from these setbacks.

This means striking the balance between driving change and maintaining continuity, sometimes called the paradox of flexibility [13].

6. *Create Short-Term Wins*

One way of building credibility is to implement changes that demonstrate you mean business. Things will change and are changing. To build credibility and secure buy in, you will need to show tangible progress and results. This is important at the outset; hence "quick wins" show your own commitment to your vision and that the program has merit.

7. *Don't Let Up*

Any transformation does not happen overnight. Your T-map will be impacted by events that have the potential to blow it off course. Plans will need to be modified, certain projects paused, and others created, as priorities change. This is completely normal. How you deal with this is your challenge as a leader. Update your T-map accordingly. Regularly take stock and reflect on advances made, how the QMS differs from say six months previously and what you need to do differently going forward. Above all, press on, and remember the connection between what you are doing and the safety and reliability of the products you are making.

8. *Making Change Stick*

The final stage of Kotter's model and certainly one that is the most difficult, is making any changes last. This is especially the case when you as a leader may move on. Will your legacy last? Will it be unpicked, and improvements begin to unravel when you are no longer there to oversee events? This is largely dependent on how well you have continuously repeated your vision and demonstrated progress versus the T-map.

The Critical Flaw in Many Improvement Plans

So, if you have leadership commitment, communicate your T-map appropriately, and generally follow a structured plan, then are you home and dry with respect to your transformational activity? Well, not quite. There is one key reason that many change programs fail and continuous improvement projects falter, both large and small and it is related to the questions: are you fixing the right problem with an appropriate solution?

Many leaders get wrapped in the messaging and the machinery of change this item gets little attention, but it is the very foundation of change. This is a critical step as your transformation will include several individual change programs and unless you have identified the root cause of an issue or opportunity correctly, you run the risk of derailing your transformation program.

A Pragmatic Approach to Root Cause Analysis

Root cause analysis (RCA) has been around for decades and is often attributable to Sakichi Toyoda one of the pioneers of Japanese manufacturing at the turn of the 20th century. RCA can be defined as a wide range of approaches, tools, and techniques used to uncover causes of problems.

The next section covers, in part, content from a multiorganizational workshop held in 2014 to distill down best practice around root cause investigation. This workshop involved a range of industry experts from organizations such as NASA, Boeing, Lockheed, and MIT [14]. The content below is pertinent only to its application to quality improvement, and certainly does not do the full publication justice.

The workshop was tasked to define a consistent approach to the rigorous application of RCA. The output covered a range of guidance and practical best practice. Specifically, it gives guidance on how the level of investigation can be scaled, dependent on the intricacy and urgency of the problem being addressed, and helps answer the question often asked: which root cause investigation tool should I use?

RCA has generally been applied to process engineering issues, but you should not confine the application to these areas. For example, why is morale in one group lower than another? Why is staff-turnover in one part of the organization greater than another? All are equally valid questions and problems that can be addressed through RCA.

One of the foundations of RCA is the assumption that there is a direct relationship between cause and effect. However, in some cases, the relationship is more complicated and will take a degree of experimentation or expert knowledge to understand. As we will cover, there are times where the link between cause and effect does not hold, or the relationship is changing. Such scenarios make the system difficult to understand, predict, and make RCA almost impossible to apply.

Root Cause Analysis Process

As in all things, it helps if you have a plan, and root cause investigation is no different. Figure 3.1 describes the high-level stages of the investigative process. It starts with defining who you need help from in getting to the answer.

1. *Team selection*
   - Appoint an individual to lead the investigation. It often helps to have somebody who isn't a subject matter expert in the process, equipment, or product in question.
   - You need a diverse team not only with skills and knowledge about the issue but also to bring in fresh eyes.
   - Bring in somebody who executes the process, not just the manager.

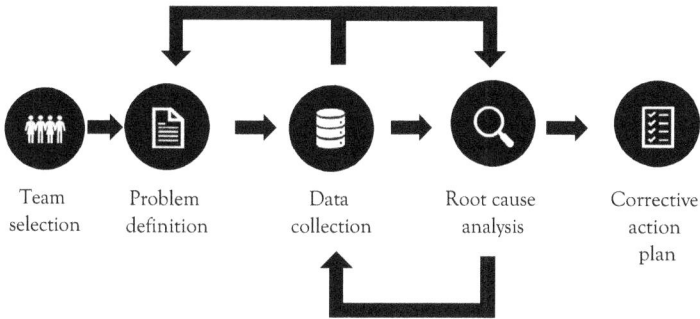

Figure 3.1 High-level stages of the root cause analysis process

- Bring in any expertise able to objectively evaluate data in an unbiased manner.
- You may need a dedicated facilitator to ensure everybody stays true to the process. Investigation facilitation is a skill, pay for it if needed.
- Finally stress that RCA isn't an exercise to apportion blame. You as a leader need to make this very clear.

2. *It starts with a problem*

   All improvements start with a problem or a metric that you want to hopefully improve. In Einstein's words "a problem defined is a problem half solved" and there is certainly merit in the belief that defining the problem is much of the battle, or conversely attempting to address the wrong problem will be wasted effort. The questions that you should ask yourself at the very beginning should include:

   - Is this the problem I need to fix? Do I need to fix it?
   - What would be gained by solving it?
   - How much effort and time resources will this require? Is it worth it?

   Unless you can clearly answer these basic questions, you will be off to a poor start. A tightly defined problem definition means you go in the right direction from the beginning. Some tips to how to do this include the following:

   - Rephrase the problem: For example, the executive asked employees to brainstorm "Ways to increase your productivity," all he got back were blank stares. When he rephrased his request as "Ways to make your jobs easier," he got a different response.

- Challenge assumptions: What are your underlying assumptions regarding the problem? Are they correct?
- Take a bird's eye view: Is this part of a bigger problem you need to address?
- Gather facts: The more information you have regarding the issue from differing perspectives the better.

Which Tool Do I Use?!

Presented with a myriad of differing tools (e.g., 5 Whys, Fishbone, Process Analysis, Cause and Effect, Timeline, etc.)—and tools that look almost identical but with differing names—it is possible to get lost on which tool is the most appropriate. Selecting the right RCA tool to use is critical and there is excellent guidance available [14].

Pitfalls of Root Cause Investigation

Ideally, if you apply some of the tools and approaches described previously, you will identify the root cause or causes of the issue you are attempting to fix. Most of the methodology is self-evident, but it is surprising how often you can be blown off course by preconceived ideas or lack of the correct expertise. The trick is to have a wide variety of expertise at the start of the investigation and bring in expertise as the root cause becomes clearer. Here are some other pitfalls you can fall into during the process and questions it helps to ask.

The Swiss cheese effect.

- Are there multiple contributing root causes that must occur simultaneously for the failure to occur? Rare events are often due to multiple events all lining up.

Target fixation.

- The team or the leader has decided the root cause at the beginning and collected data to support this known theory.

- Was the evaluation truly unbiased and objective?
- Is there evidence that contradicts the root cause that is being ignored?
- Do you need to refresh the team with new sets of eyes to get another perspective?

Incorrect data classification.

- Is the investigation based on assumptions rather than objective evidence?

Root Cause Analysis Applied to the QMS

In practice, over the past 20 years, a lot of investigational tools have been applied in organizations and are now being shoehorned into the QMS. These approaches work well with discrete problems related to specific issues. Their use can be less effective in circumstances where you need to look more strategically, as is the case with a QMS transformation. This issue is related to both the breadth and depth of their use in the QMS.

Breadth

One of the issues with RCA in the context of the QMS is that it can lead to a blinkered approach. Often, we are keen to address very specific issues as one-time events and do not see the association between similar issues. These may not manifest themselves in the same way but are essentially the same problem.

Depth

One of the failures in all investigations is not drilling down sufficiently to get to the true root cause. Often the investigator has little influence in implementing deeper fixes, as this involves areas outside the investigator's authority and means asking broader questions. For example, do you have the right expertise within your company? Is the quality organization orga-nized effectively, and what is the culture of quality within your business? However, if you as a leader do not address some of these more systemic causes, then you will continually have to address the issues as they manifest themselves as individual events. You will need to ask deeper questions to identify the true change you need to make.

Whatever approach you take your decisions will generally be based on review of data, and a particular type of data, Quality Data.

Quality Data

Quality Data is data generated through the execution of the QMS. It can be quantitative or qualitative/narrative.

Whatever the type of data you use, the integrity of Quality Data is critical. Its analysis is used for the baseline performance of the QMS and to determine if improvements are needed. Quality Data is used as the basis of data-driven decisions around performance of the QMS. As such, Quality Data requires specific controls on how the data is collected, presented, analyzed, and verified as accurate. Your biggest danger will be making the wrong decisions based on incomplete or incorrect data.

Quality Data should be appropriately presented in a visual manner to aid understanding and support any conclusion derived from the dataset. As always, a picture can speak a thousand words.

Prioritization

All change competes with other activities. The danger is that in taking too much on, nothing of merit is achieved. Owing to the authority that leaders have over their organizations, individuals and groups may agree to make things happen, even if they are fully aware that these commitments cannot be delivered. The role of the leader is to help the organizations decide which activities have greater benefit than the effort required to deliver them. This is often rarely considered, particularly with respect to changes in the quality system. One tool to help in applying a degree of objectivity such that the pros and cons of change can be compared is the Benefit versus Effort grid (see Figure 3.2).

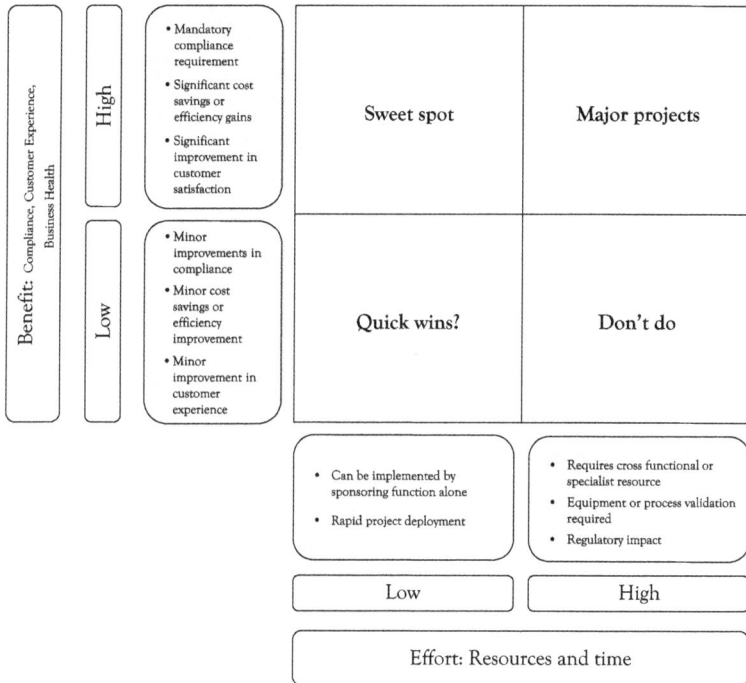

Figure 3.2 *Benefit versus Effort grid*

The use of this Benefit versus Effort approach has several benefits:

- It allows direct comparison between activities in an objective manner, such that the "squeaky wheel" does not always get the oil.
- It allows activities that have clear no-brainer benefits to go ahead immediately.
- It focuses you to really assess whether activities have the benefits expected.
- It allows a degree of prioritization of items, allowing the activity to be placed in a queue to be delivered when resources become available.

Such methodology and approach are nothing new but often forgotten when improvements to the QMS are considered. The approach described previously is valuable to filter changes prior to management in the change control process, whether through an electronic application or a paper-based system.

Summary

Customer-focused continuous improvement is the bedrock of a successful QMS.

- A quality system that fails to change is one that will fail to meet its customer needs.
- Ask yourself what is holding your quality system back from meeting customer needs?
- Change management is far more than just document control.
- Make sure you are addressing the correct causes with the right fixes.
- Prioritize benefit against effort before progressing.

CHAPTER 4

Risk

Intelligence Won't Protect You

By all accounts the sea was calm, and though overcast, visibility was good. It should have been a simple maneuver; one he had completed many times before. On January 13, 2012—Francesco Schettino—Captain of the cruise liner Costa Concordia attempted to perform a sail-past of the local town. It ended in disaster [15].

The ship struck rocks along the island of Giglio and was holed. Within minutes it was taking in water and listing badly. In the ensuing mayhem, 32 people lost their lives. As part of the resulting investigation, several contributory factors were identified—including the captain's less-than-textbook response to the event. But principally, the captain's actions were concluded to be at fault. He was sentenced to 16 years in jail. His maritime career was effectively over, his personal and professional reputation in tatters.

You don't become the Captain of a cruise liner by mistake. There are exams to pass and qualifications that you must achieve, in addition years of competence you need to demonstrate as you work your way up the career ladder. Francesco Schettino certainly wasn't an unintelligent man but looking back he made a tragically poor decision.

Why?

Maybe, despite his intelligence, he simply made a poor call? But there is a growing body of evidence that rather than preventing you making a bad decision, both experience and intelligence can contribute to making terrible decisions. In addition, the cleverer you are and the more experience you have, the worse your decision making can become and the greater the consequences when you get it wrong.

Some would say that Schettino just had a bit of bad luck. In your position you will also encounter a number of issues that you will put down to bad luck. Conversely, items that are essentially good luck you will class as achievements, the result of your intelligence and your extensive experience. How often have you owned up to that correct call you made, being nothing more than a guess?

The painful truth is that intelligence will not protect you from bad luck or even making terrible decisions. History is littered with intelligent people making poor calls.

So, what can help you when a poor quality decision can have disastrous consequences impacting people's lives?

There is one area that can shield you from bad luck and making poor calls: risk management.

But only if you apply it correctly. Only if you apply it in an objective, distanced, and humble way.

William James, the 19th-century philosopher once stated: "A great many people think they are thinking when they are merely rearranging their prejudices."

The problem isn't so much the tools, it's us as we try to apply them. As a leader you're probably reading this with a quite distinct idea of what risk management means and how it should be applied. True, some of the tools we will cover are not new, but essentially the application of risk management *is* the purpose of quality management.

However, knowing which tools to apply will not completely protect you from making bad calls. Virtually every product that has been recalled had, at some point in its life cycle, risk management rigorously applied to its design, manufacture, and distribution. The question isn't so much, what you apply, it is how you apply it.

The Trap of Intelligence

David Robson in his 2020 publication *The Intelligence Trap* makes a well-made argument, supported by a wide range of psychological research, that intelligence itself comes with its own baggage and drawbacks [16]. Principally, those we would generally consider to be intelligent, have personal biases like the rest of us. Importantly, they are better able to use their intelligence to argue their position is right, even when it is patently wrong. In effect, the more intelligent you are, the less able you are to recognize flaws in your own thinking, and better able to convince others you are correct. But it goes beyond that.

Those that we would consider to be experts in their respective fields often feel they have legitimacy of opinion outside their original field. How often have you seen leaders during a crisis or technical challenge begin to proffer their own opinions outside areas that they have competence, rather than allowing the appropriate technical experts to lead?

Robson makes the critical point that it's not so much that intelligence is useful, any more than knowledge is, but it is how it is applied practically for best use: wisdom.

As a leader you may have data, information, and knowledge available, but it is your wisdom that is going to keep your business and customers from harm. You'll also need some structure to ensure your assessment of risk is objective as it can be.

Components of Risk

Safety is defined with respect to risk management as: the absence of *unacceptable* risk. But what is unacceptable and who decides it? Note the definition does not say absence of all risk. Zero risk is unattainable. Another aspect of risk management is that our tolerance of risk can change. New information can arise or a better understanding of current risks emerges.

One of the core principles of risk management is that somebody must decide what is an unacceptable risk. But risk can be very personal, which is a challenge when you try to standardize approaches to managing it.

Central to risk management methodology is the concept of hazard and harm. Table 4.1 details the concepts of how hazards, through the generation of hazardous situations, can form the potential for harm, which in turn can cause harm.

Table 4.1 Examples of hazard, hazardous situation, and harm for a diagnostic product

Hazard	Hazardous Situation	Harm
Lack of batch homogeneity	Inaccurate results	Incorrect patient diagnosis
Accidental damage	Sharp surface	Physical injury
Inadequate instructions	Diagnostic is unclear	Delay in patient treatment

Essentially risk is a product of how bad something could be—severity of the harm—and the probability of it happening. Let's look at these two components of severity and probability of harm in more detail.

Severity

Severity effectively means how bad something could be. It helps to categorize the different levels of severity. International standards define severity as the measurement of the *possible consequences* of the hazard (harm).

This obviously raises the question of severity of harm to what? Is it customer health? Compliance status? Financial consequences? Generally, risk models have focused on health.

Table 4.2 provides a severity scale from one to five going from negligible to catastrophic. In this example, the impact is to patient health for a medical device.

There are two aspects of the definition of severity that are very important. The first one is around the word "possible." The consequence of harm needs to be credible. It can be very unlikely, but it needs to be credible. For example, when looking at the risk of a manufacturing line breaking down, one failure mode could be the production floor being hit by a meteorite. This however is not a credible event. It is an incredible event.

The second aspect is that the severity classification should be based on the presumption that the harm will occur, even if you may decide the probability is very unlikely. The two components of severity and probability of harm are treated independently and ideally, one should not pollute the other.

Table 4.2 Example of levels of severity for a medical device

Level	Severity	Impact
5	Catastrophic	Harm to patient/user: Requires emergency surgery. May cause permanent injury or death.
4	Critical	Harm to patient/user: Requires medical or surgical intervention.
3	Major	Harm to patient/user: Able to be cured with minor treatment.
2	Minor	Potential for harm to the patient/user.
1	Negligible	No potential for harm to the patient/user. Inconvenience.

The estimation of severity should also be based on the presumption that no mitigation will take place, even though you know this will occur. In practice, the easiest way of classifying severity is to simply answer the question: "What is the worst that would happen if I hadn't/don't detect this issue?"

It is very tempting to overanalyze. A good tip is that if you can quickly answer the above question, generally you'll be in the right area regarding classifying the severity.

Probability of Harm

In the same way as the severity component, it is possible to create a sliding scale of probability of harm from improbable to frequent (see Table 4.3). Unlike severity estimation the probability component is more difficult to assess. Often data won't be available to make an accurate determination of the probability of occurrence. It can help to use historical data from similar products, processes, or changes if available. Though, essentially, the probability estimate is at times little more than an educated guess. Essentially you need to answer the question: "How likely is it that the harm would occur?"

In most risk management models these two components that is, severity and probability of occurrence of harm, are combined to create an overall risk score. This may be a number or a more qualitative estimate of risk.

Table 4.3 Example of levels of probability of harm

Level	Probability of Occurrence	Frequency
5	Frequent	Hazard occurs frequently. Would not be surprising if it occurred ≥ 1 in 100 occasions.
4	Probable	Hazard occurs consistently at a low frequency. Would not be surprised if it occurred < 1 in 100 and ≥ 1 in 1,000.
3	Possible	Hazard has the potential to occur. Would be surprised if it occurred < 1 in 1,000 and ≥ 1 in 10,000.
2	Remote	Hazard has the potential to occur. Would be surprised if it occurred < 1 in 10,000 and ≥ 1 in 100,000.
1	Improbable	Hazard has an extremely remote potential to occur. Would be surprised if it occurred < 1 in 100,000.

Figure 4.1 gives an example of such a risk matrix. Based on the product of these two components, a determination can be made whether the risk is Acceptable, Unacceptable, or simply Undesirable. This leads to one of the biggest challenges with the application of risk management that is, defining the boundary between the risk levels and the appropriate response.

Generally, in organizations such as healthcare, this determination is carried out with multiple inputs from the leadership team, the Quality organization, and those who know how the final product will be used, such as clinicians. Often this classification is validated using case studies to determine whether the regions of risk acceptability are credible and feel valid and appropriate. The organization also must decide the applicable response for each region.

Unacceptable risks mandate a degree of control measures to be implemented to reduce the risks to an acceptable level and move it from this Unacceptable zone. Undesirable risks, generally, require that the risk is reduced if practical. Usually risks that land in the Acceptable zone are considered to be sufficiently low such that they require no further mitigation. Generally, the risk management methodology described previously is to focus effort and resources on risks that are deemed Unacceptable or Undesirable.

This two-component concept is the basis of many of the risk management models currently in use, with probability on one axis and the

Probability of Harm						
Frequent	5	Unacceptable	Unacceptable	Unacceptable	Unacceptable	Unacceptable
Probable	4	Undesirable	Undesirable	Unacceptable	Unacceptable	Unacceptable
Possible	3	Acceptable	Undesirable	Undesirable	Unacceptable	Unacceptable
Remote	2	Acceptable	Acceptable	Undesirable	Undesirable	Unacceptable
Improbable	1	Acceptable	Acceptable	Acceptable	Undesirable	Undesirable
Severity		1	2	3	4	5
		Negligible	Minor	Major	Critical	Catastrophic

Figure 4.1 Example of a risk matrix

impact/severity of the issue on another and the product of these two components being considered: risk.

Risk Reduction

In order to implement risk reduction activities, certain risk management standards such as ISO14971—for medical devices—give requirements on the priority of activities to be considered when risk needs to be reduced to acceptable levels that is, inherently safe by design and manufacture >> protective measures >> information and training.

Risk is ideally reduced through implementation of controls that ensure the product is inherently safe by design and manufacture. First, the device is ensured safe by implementation of appropriate design controls to ensure the product fulfills design requirements and all customer and regulatory expectations. Secondly, consistent and safe manufacture, and post market surveillance is ensured through the execution of an effective QMS to ensure that risks are reduced.

Protective measures are the next preferred port of call, measures in the product itself or in the manufacturing process to detect failures. These include alarms, control systems during manufacturing, product inspection, and release tests.

The final control measures to be considered are the weakest and simply increase awareness of potential failures occurring through use of the product. These include instructions for use, warnings, labeling, operator training, and so on.

In terms of reducing harm, harm does not necessarily always mean harm to human health. It could be harm to an organization's compliance status. It could be harm to its financial health. In a similar way to how the QMS can be seen to have three principal customers: customer experience, regulatory compliance, and business health, each of these aspects could also be harmed in different ways.

In essence, the main role of a quality professional is balancing the risk of harm to these three components. So, which of these components takes priority and how can this balance between the three be achieved and what does this mean in practice?

Balancing Risks

The principal focus is virtually always the impact of changes to the product, with particular focus on health and safety. This focus on health is reflected in the numerous regulations and standards regarding risk management within the healthcare industry.

As we covered previously, changes may also impact other aspects of the business influenced by the QMS. These three areas are not, however, equally weighted with respect to importance. As a generalization, Safety concerns—that is, not harming health, take priority over Compliance—that is, not breaking the law, which takes precedence over Business Health that is, being profitable.

We would, however, argue that while certainly never the main driver, cost is not irrelevant. Extensive risk reduction activities come at a price to implement; a price sometimes disproportionate to the risk being mitigated.

Often a quality professional is reluctant to engage in the concept of cost, profit, and aspects of the balance sheet, uncomfortable that cost would ever sway their decision process. Often these behaviors are due to lack of experience, lack of confidence in their own decision-making abilities, and absence of leadership support.

For the Quality profession to survive, the industry needs to embrace the concept that the real role of the Quality professional is balancing risk and working through areas of uncertainty, grayness, and to help the organization address sometimes messy and uncomfortable problems.

Seek Diverse Opinions

To adequately assess risk, you will need the right people in the room. Generally, diversity is a good thing. The danger in assessing risk, like all collective decision making, is the consensus view arrived at can be one that meets nobody's needs. The consensus average may simply be too far from the truth. Often it does not recognize outlier opinions as credible. A skillful facilitator needs to ensure that all valid opinions are reflected, and all-potential credible risks are considered.

This however poses a dilemma as outlier voices are not generally tolerated. In addition, a melee of diverse opinions can lead to a degree of paralysis, as decisions are not made and the process stalls.

The way to address these two dilemmas is to not only acknowledge that diverse opinions are welcome and valid but also agree beforehand how final decisions will be made. The process may be by majority vote, be the responsibility of the individual running the risk assessment exercise or elevated up the management chain for final arbitration. All these approaches are equally valid, but it does require a clear predetermined approach that everybody supports to prevent the process becoming bogged down.

The issue of individuals and functions within the risk management process is complex. Often risk assessments are viewed as no more than paper exercises for compliance purposes, the generation of which will make the specific, inconvenient issue go away.

So how do we stop this happening?

First, we need to ensure that all individuals involved in the process are aware of their own potential biases. Secondly, remind everybody that risk is being assessed to get to the truth to best protect the customer.

Remember that for every defective product that escaped the production system, for every product recall and every supply chain challenge, there is usually a risk assessment that had been completed in accordance with the regulations.

Overestimating Risk

Let's consider probability of harm. In the absence of any supporting data, it is not uncommon to construct scenarios that are improbable. Do not clutter your risk assessment with fantasy scenarios that are so unlikely that putting mitigations in place is a waste of time. The trick is to be able to separate the incredible from the improbable.

Regarding the severity component, it is also easy to overestimate the risk. It is very easy to forget the checks and balances in place within your business that prevent defective material from escaping or it being used incorrectly.

The risk management standards do not specifically call out your ability to detect and contain defects, but it is embedded in the parameter of probability of harm, but do not overlook this aspect to contain defects. Again, you need to answer the question: "What is the worst that would happen if I hadn't detected/don't detect this issue?"

Underestimating Risk

One of the main failings of the application of risk management is its use to justify why everything is in control, when it's not. Its purpose is to expose legitimate weaknesses in product, processes, and systems. The worst example of this can be seen how risk management is applied to the assessment of nonconformances.

Many organizations have a nonconformance or deviation process in place to react to either defective product or deviations from the expectations of their quality system. Often, risk management is incorporated into the process to stratify and focus activity on items that are higher risk, rather than those that are trivial and inconsequential. This is sensible and highly laudable. But sometimes it can be applied incorrectly and the fact that the nonconformance has been found used as justification that the risk is low, as the issue has been contained. This is important. Getting the risk evaluation wrong can have huge consequences. It is more than a documentation issue.

The mitigations to prevent your QMS generating such misclassifications include appropriate qualification/validation of your risk management methodology and effective training and assessment during deployment of risk management techniques. Critically, there should be an expectation that senior management take a close interest in how risk management is applied within your organizations.

Snapshots in Time

One of the deficiencies of risk management, which is merely a reflection of how it's applied, is that it can only be a snapshot based on the information available at the time. Risk assessments are typically treated as one-time events, completed, signed off, and filed in the documentation system. This is not how they should be treated.

Risk assessments should be viewed as a "living document." It is surprising how seldom organizations update product risk management plans, or even view them periodically for adequacy. Process-driven rules should drive risk assessment activities, be it product risk assessments or failure modes effects analysis (FMEA), for any significant process change.

It should also document—with rationale—why certain risks do not require risk mitigation. Justifying why you will not do something is as important as promising you will.

Risk Management Tools

There are two principal risk management tools. There is the risk assessment template, the precise format of which depends on which industry you are in and the standards that apply (e.g., ISO 14791:2019, which is applicable to the medical device industry).

Secondly, there is a tool that is generally applied to assess process reliability called FMEA. This tool differs from the previous template in that the probability of harm is generally split out into two further components that is, probability of occurrence and probability of detection.

Sometimes there is confusion on which tool to apply. Auditors assessing compliance against risk management standards generally require formats of risk assessment that comply with the former template, while engineers generally see the FMEA as the "go-to" tool for assessing risk.

The standards and regulations expect that risk be assessed using methods aligned with the ISO standard applicable to your industry. There are, however, certain cases where FMEA is more appropriate to assess risk and quantifying the reliability of a process. There are also scenarios where both approaches may be used or an FMEA leads to update of the relevant risk management plans. In essence, both tools have differing purposes as described in Table 4.4.

Table 4.4 Differences between classical management of risk approaches and FMEA

Classical Management of Risk e.g., ISO14971: 2019	FMEA e.g., IEC60812: 2018
Is used early in the design process and starts with identifying hazards.	Is used late in the design process. A detailed process map is already available.
Considers risk from normal use, unintended use, and failure.	Considers only failures.
Severity is generally based on harm to the patient.	Severity can be based on multiple features e.g.: safety, cost, and compliance.
Used to manage all risks.	Is focused on assessing and improving reliability.

Tips for Applying Risk Management Within the QMS

Learn From Your Past

One of the common features of virtually all disasters is that the system was "blinking red" well before the event. From the Deepwater Horizon catastrophe in 2010, where an oil-platform blowout caused the greatest environmental catastrophe in history to the Shuttle Columbia disaster in 2003, near miss events preceded the eventual failure. In all cases, the signs were there in the system. Previous near-miss incidents occurred, which would have prevented loss of life if they had been heeded [17].

For organizations that do not react to signals in the quality system (e.g., near misses, complaints, etc.), these signals become "noise" and the risk tolerance of the organization shifts significantly without it knowing, until eventually, disaster strikes [18]. This was one of the key findings of the National Commission on the BP Deepwater Horizon Oil Spill and Offshore Drilling [19].

Organizations that set high expectations of individuals to raise their hands and react to near miss events are more protected, but only when leadership actively supports this.

Do Not Undermine Trust

A key requirement for transforming a Quality organization is the expectation that individuals highlight areas that require improvement. This transparency works both ways. As a business leader, you need to be open and honest with the organization. Expectations not being met is not a sign of failure. Failure is not being honest about the reality of challenges and course correcting as needed as unexpected risks appear. Successful organizations learn from their failures [20].

Proportionality

One of the consequences of stratifying issues based on risk is that you do not treat all events the same. You may not even react to low-risk events.

While at the other end of the risk continuum you need to respond with urgency, apply significant resources and focus on events that are of high risk to your customers, business, or compliance status.

If you operate a quality system of extreme stringency, then you will create a system that is overly bureaucratic, resource hungry, and slow to react. Ironically, it will not always ensure that you are in full compliance, or the customer protected, as procedures become a challenge to follow. You will become lost in a myriad of compliance requirements, many of which have little to do with meeting customer expectations.

At the other extreme, if you operate a system that is too hands off, eventually you will pay the price as issues are not fixed and the QMS becomes a significant compliance risk.

As a leader, you set the level of stringency. For example, if a record verifying the floor has been swept is not signed, or a batch record has a minor error. Is each occurrence worthy of a formal nonconformance and investigation? Possibly. Though it may be more pragmatic to review each event and react when a pattern emerges or systemic issues identified. Maybe coach individuals who are making errors before adding the issue to the QMS. Do not overfeed the system. It will not cope. React with proportionality.

This may be a challenge as making calls in quality is never easy, due to one aspect: the grayness.

It's a Gray Area and Sometimes You'll Get It Wrong

Quality involves handling degrees of probability, and probability by its very definition does not equate to certainty. Judgment calls are made based on degrees of confidence. While these levels of confidence may be high that is, 95 or 99 percent, this does not mean decisions and consequences are absolute. Add in incidents that are atypical and hence do not follow the rules of probability, one thing is certain. The quality professional will at times make a call that, with hindsight, is totally wrong. Consequently, if you want a job where there are never bad consequences of your decisions, then a job as a Quality professional is not for you. Conversely, if you want a job that involves protecting the patient from harm, growing the business, and one where your day-to-day actions are rewarding, then maybe it is a job for you. It is a job as much about people, as about data.

Every decision a quality professional makes is generally one based on balance of risk. Sometimes data is absent, assumptions are incorrect, and wrong decisions are made. As a leader of an effective Quality organization, you need to ensure that individuals are comfortable making wrong decisions.

This comes with one critical caveat. Do they learn from mistakes? Do they subsequently ask the questions: Why was my decision not correct? What would I do differently next time? What information was lacking? Why was my assumption incorrect? Key is the ability to think critically and reflect.

As a leader you will need to foster a culture of prudent risk taking, based on data-driven decisions. The alternative to such an approach is organizational paralysis, which is often worse than making a suboptimal decision. At times you will have to put aside your own assumptions, prejudices, and ego. You will need to accept at times you don't know or have all the answers. This does take at times a degree of steadfastness and self-belief.

Break Down Information Barriers

Anybody can make a decision based on a hunch, gut feeling, or simply a guess. In the real world, however, you must explain decisions to business partners, stakeholders, and regulators. You will need data to support your decisions, and there lies one part of the problem. The data is not always available at your fingertips when it is needed.

That is, not to say, having access to information will always drive appropriate decision making. Sometimes information is requested to give credence to decisions that have already been made. But a large degree of protection against abuse of information is gained through critical thinking and reflection. As a leader you need to make sure your organization has the right information, in the right hands, and people are using it to make the right decisions.

Summary

Risk management *is* quality management.

- Effective risk management is your only protection against making stupid and bad decisions that will harm your business.
- Understand the inherent risks within the risk management process that is, bias and overconfidence.
- Embrace diversity of opinion. Temper with critical thinking and reflection.
- Learn to differentiate between data, information, knowledge, and wisdom.
- Document, document, document. Revise, revise, revise.
- Your risk assessment should be one of your most frequently reviewed resources.

CHAPTER 5

Worldviews and the QMS

Systems Thinking

How we view the world around us is key to all aspects of our professional and personal lives. It helps you make sense of the world around you; defines how you interact with it and helps define how you believe it behaves. One feature of the improvement methodology described in the previous chapter is that it assumes the world functions as a machine. Inputs can be controlled, outputs can be measured, and there is a fundamental link between cause and effect. Even the concept of root cause infers that there can be one, or several, foundational causes of problems; be they defective units of production, delays in manufacturing, customer dissatisfaction, noncompliance against procedures, or even product recalls.

Engineers and scientists will invariably approach such challenges with a reductionistic mindset, one that has been reenforced through a lifetime of training and experience.

But is this really the case? Do organizations and people really behave like machines?

Consider where you were 5 to 10 years ago. Where was your business? Where was your personal life? Did the events and expectations over the past years play out exactly as you expected? Of course not, they seldom do, and it isn't for the want of planning and preparation. The reason things generally don't go quite as expected is that the world isn't a machine. It is a complex moving process. Unexpected things happen, which lead to other events. This is called life. So why do we treat processes, organizations, and factories very differently, with an expectation that they behave like automatons we can always control?

> Organizations may be in constant turmoil due to reorganizations, change of personnel, fluctuations in leadership style … or turbulence as a consequence of market and customers.
>
> —Øgland, Petter (2008) [21]

In reality, the environment in which we attempt to execute continuous improvement is constantly changing and moving. It sometimes puts into question whether these approaches are always valid or as predictable as we think. Undeterred, process engineers realized that the simplistic reductionistic view at the individual process level needed to be broadened to encompass whole systems of connected processes. We will see in a later chapter that this wasn't the complete answer. While we recognize that organizations and the world in general appear to be in constant flux, we continue to apply approaches that require order, stability, and clear cause and effect. Despite this paradox looking at systems was a significant step forward.

Systems Thinking

Over the years, ways of looking at processes has evolved into a more systems approach. Since its inception in the 1990s, systems thinking has been applied to settings ranging from healthcare to addressing social challenges.

A fundamental principle of systems thinking is that improvement cannot be made unless the underlying system is addressed and "a system's failure requires a system solution" [22]. Over the last 20 years, systems thinking has evolved from more traditional process views to better explain—though not completely—how the world operates. It can be found being applied in the public sector, schools, local authorities, and large businesses.

A systems approach is seen by many as key in addressing the quality challenges in delivering appropriate healthcare [22].

Systems Thinking and Governmental Policy Making

If you think your job as a leader is challenging, think how it must be if your responsibility is running a whole economy or shaping how society reacts to a critical public health emergency?

In recent times, there have been two challenges that help demonstrate how looking at the system can inform, and hopefully predict the most appropriate solution to some of society's most intractable problems.

The U.S. Opioid Crisis

Since the late 1990s, forms of synthetic opiates have often been recommended for the treatment of severe pain. Sadly, their use has resulted in a wave of deaths due to huge numbers of overdoses, as the drugs became overprescribed by the medical community.

Looking back with the benefit of hindsight, we can now see society's reaction to these deaths as one of abject failure. It is one that has claimed thousands of lives in the past 20 years.

Initially, the appropriate response to the deaths was obvious: restrict the supply of the drugs. Subsequently, prescribing opiate derivatives was curtailed, to help bring the death rate under control.

Sadly, the problem did not go away. Addicts turned to the use of illegal heroin bought on the street once their physicians refused to support their addiction, one that they in many cases had helped start. This caused a second wave in deaths, as patients turned to these illegal forms of the drug. Currently we are in the midst of a third wave of fatalities, the result of both prescription drugs and illicitly manufactured opioid derivatives now becoming available.

Looking back, now we can see that the initial reaction to the opioid crisis was an example of machine thinking, controlling inputs, and expecting different outputs. The Food and Drug Administration (FDA) in the United States began to conclude that another strategy was needed. They decided that such an approach was naïve, and the crisis required:

> multiple interventions, products, technologies, policies, and communications—working together [23].

The FDA began to embrace systems thinking to create a model, better predictive of more successful interventions. They recognized that the crisis:

- Was heterogenous: The social, physiological, and organizational interactions were hard to predict and the underlying mechanism difficult to fully understand.
- Had multiple stakeholders: No single authority had complete jurisdiction.
- There is a delay in system between any intervention and seeing an impact.
- Sometimes interventions resulted in outcomes that were unexpected, counter to the result predicted and hoped for.
- Was evolving.
- Had data gaps limited understanding of knowledge.

Reducing availability of prescription opioids had unexpected consequences. It made the situation worse, as patients went to extreme lengths to obtain medication by legal and often illegal means. Understanding the impact of interventions was difficult with multiple stakeholders at play with different perspectives and their own personal measures of success. These ranged from the media, law enforcement agencies, healthcare providers to community leaders. The effort required to fully understand the system, and the consequences of taking a reductionistic approach was literally a matter of life and death.

The FDA began to create a systems model of the opioid crisis to better predict outcomes of suitable interventions. They began to explore approaches such as mandatory education on the dangers of opioids for prescribers; allowing greater access to medicines to reverse the symptoms of overdose and supporting research into better pain management.

It is too early to determine whether these broader more systemic approaches will be successful, but it will not be for the want of looking at this healthcare challenge through a more holistic lens.

More broadly, the FDA also understands your organization is a system, your business is a system and your QMS is a system. The approaches that the FDA are taking will eventually translate into an expectation of organizations to use such strategies to protect the consumer and ensure that products are manufactured that are safe.

Certainly, one example of how systems operate within healthcare, one we can all relate to is the global response to the greatest public health challenge faced by society in the last 50 years that is, the Covid-19 pandemic.

Covid-19 Pandemic

The Covid-19 pandemic of 2020–2021 was a clear example of the inter-connected nature of our society, healthcare systems, and economies on a global scale. It also highlighted an essential component of systems think-ing with actions resulting in often unexpected and unintended conse-quences. Through the implementation of control measures such as social distancing, local lockdowns, and implementation of personal protective equipment several negative impacts occurred. These ranged from mental health challenges, lack of treatment of many life-threatening noncovid conditions, and even an increase in domestic violence. The impact of these control measures is still being felt on disparate sections of society, the political landscape, and the economy. The connected nature of these systems was brought into sharp focus during the pandemic [24].

Even looking at one small aspect of the pandemic that is, society's response to the spread of the virus and attempts to contain it, the interac-tions and feedback loops are extensive and reinforce again how connected the real world is (see Figure 5.1).

From these two examples it is clear that the real world does not oper-ate as a collection of disconnected processes, but as a system. Your orga-nization is no different. Now is the time to start applying such systems thinking to management of quality, particularly within healthcare.

A system is not just a collection of processes. A system is holistic, and you cannot understand the system without looking at the totality of the system. By its very definition a QMS is a *system*, but not always viewed as such. Often, each part of the QMS is seen as separate, each with its own procedures and documentation. In practice, all aspects of the QMS are interconnected to a greater or lesser degree. Not viewing them as a system has consequences.

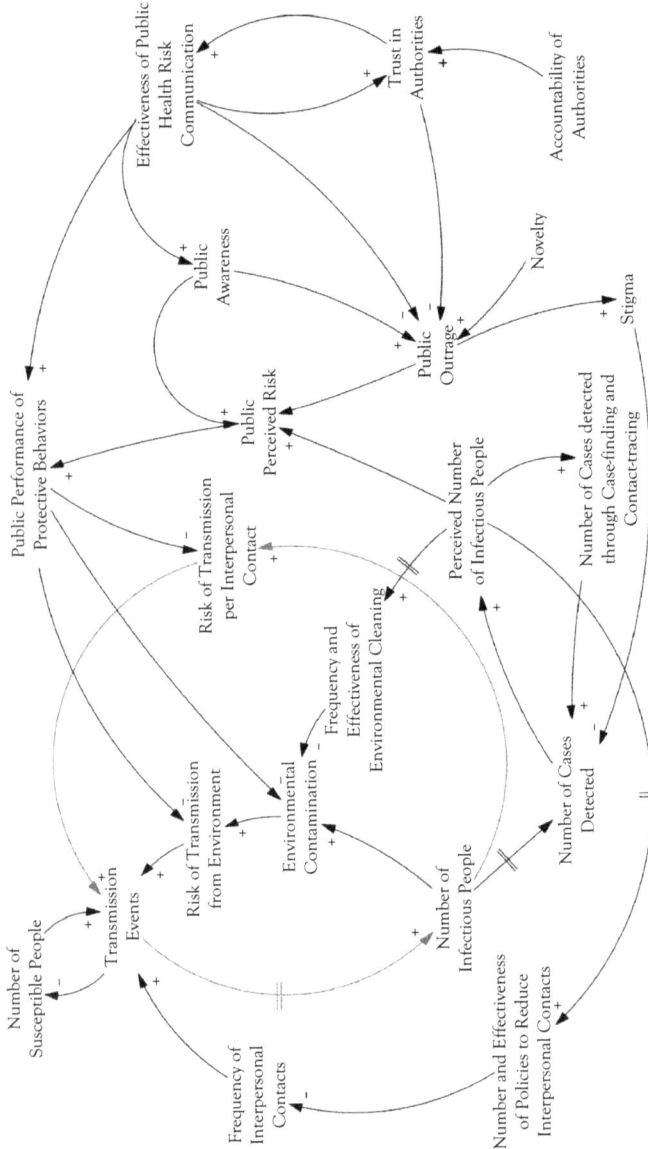

Figure 5.1 An example causal loop diagram illustrating some of the interacting components in a society responding to the threat of Covid-19 [24]

In 2003, John Seddon proposed a model for checking a system and offers some structure to help comprehend one in action [25].

The model comprises six attributes:

- Purpose
- Demand
- Capability
- Flow
- System Conditions
- Management Thinking

In the following, we will explore how these attributes manifest themselves in the QMS.

Purpose: What Is the Purpose of the System?

The answer to this question may depend on who the customers of the system are, and their specific needs. For example, is the CAPA system in place to fix and prevent errors and to continually improve the QMS, or to create documents to demonstrate to an auditor you have a CAPA process that meets the regulations? These are two different things, though often confounded.

Demand: What Are the Demands on the System?

Every system has demand put on it. The QMS is no different. There are two types of demand, Value Demand, which is demand aligned with the purpose of the system, and Failure Demand. Failure Demand is demand caused by failure to deliver something right for the customer. Errors in manufacturing records are a form of Failure Demand and cause unnecessary rework in other parts of the system. Incomplete or poorly defined customer design inputs create Failure Demand during product development, as product is potentially redesigned before or even after its launch.

In some organizations work generated by the QMS can give the illusion that the system is working. In reality it may be completely delinked and detracting from fulfilling final customer needs. The system creates its own work delinked from meeting customer expectations. Reports are created that are never read. Data compiled that is never reviewed or data reviewed with no decision reached.

Ask yourself the question: how much daily activity within your QMS is delivering against customer expectations around customer experience, compliance, and business health?

Capability: Is the System Capable of Meeting the Load Put on It?

How will your quality system meet peaks of demand or events such as product recalls or external audits that put sudden urgent stress on the system and its human resources?

Flow: How Does the System Flow to Meet Demand?

The system is not static but needs to flow to meet demand. During the product realization process, how do your records, documents, and data flow with the product? How is this managed if different systems, such as electronic batch records, enterprise resource planning applications, e-QMS as well as the physical product and paperwork need to move in unison?

System Conditions: What Causes the System to Behave as It Does?

Often subsystems are misaligned. One example of systems that are often not aligned are the two subsystems of the QMS: Design Control and Product Realization.

Through the process of Design Control, new products designed by R&D are eventually handed over to the factory accountable for making them. Often the success criteria for this handover is measured by whether the product was launched on time and the relevant regulatory approval obtained.

This process is never error free. Through the generation of procedures that are unclear and the design of products with poor capability, products are often handed over that require rework or incur excessive scrap during the manufacturing process. These teething problems require fixing. Many an operational director has taken ownership of products prematurely but has taken one for the team. The product is launched on time, but with an ongoing cost. Post launch, the CAPA system generally clears up this mess to improve the capability of product and/or quality of the documentation and the system settles back down.

Often there is little real learning from this exercise. Information is not fed back into the design process to ensure that subsequent products are better designed. The two processes, while theoretically joined at the hip in the QMS, are often delinked with respect to aligned success metrics, owners, and accountability. The system behaves as it was created, with errors and in a disjointed way.

Management Thinking: Are Your Managers Focused on the Customers or Just Satisfying Your Needs?

Systems do not operate on their own. They take people, and people are driven by beliefs and behaviors that make up organizational culture. Often, the behavior of the system is simply a function of those who run and manage it. This comes down to more nebulous aspects of the QMS that forms the foundation of how it behaves and is executed. Aspects that are difficult to measure often have a huge impact.

A Systems Approach to Quality Management in Healthcare

The healthcare setting has been described as well suited to the application of systems thinking [26]. Poor quality has real potential for patient harm through human error or inappropriate application of medicine or procedures. This is often the result of critical information moving between groups, unclear ownership of processes, and often the absence of a recognized team that would aid collaborative working. Sound familiar? These may be aspects you recognize in your Quality organization.

Underlying Causes

One of the key concepts of systems thinking is one of underlying causes as demonstrated in the iceberg model [27]. In summary, the model proposes that while most problems and issues may manifest themselves above the waterline, the majority of causes are found below the water. We may address events with knee-jerk reactions, but unless we address the more foundational causes, such as individual behavior and viewpoints, then implementing change that is sustainable and one that will be long lasting will always be wanting (see Figure 5.2.).

The concept of layers of causes can be explored with respect to an event that is not uncommon in the healthcare industry: a product recall.

Owing to the complex nature of healthcare products, recalls within these regulated industries are not unusual. In fact, the absence of recalls can be a sign that the QMS is ineffective and not reacting appropriately to signals. The expectation of regulators is that businesses act swiftly when products do not meet claims and may pose a risk to patient safety.

A recall is generally a reactive event. Essentially, recalls represent defects that have escaped the controls and containment of the quality system. They rarely happen out of the blue with no warning. Often these events are preceded by other issues, ones caught by simple good fortune: the chance observation by an individual on the production line that something did not look quite right or the error spotted in the batch record through chance. Some organizations call these "near miss" events or "close calls." These are often viewed as a special type of deviation in the QMS, which is telling the business something important. They demonstrate a weakness in the containment system. One that wasn't breached through nothing more than good luck.

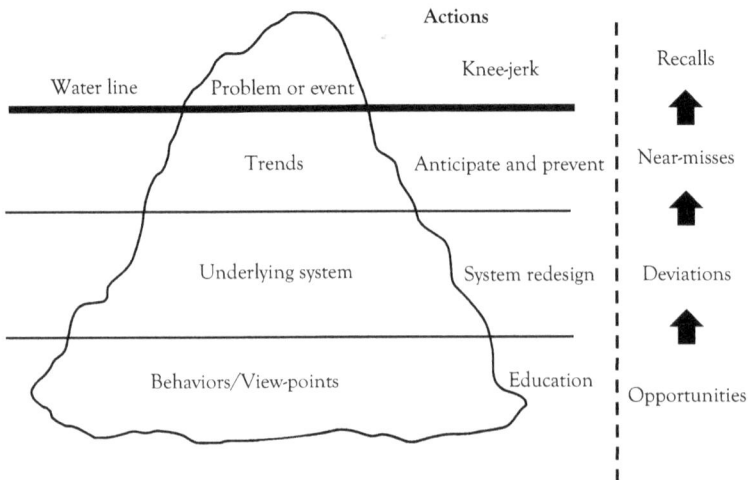

Figure 5.2 An example of the iceberg model of causes

Preceding these near misses there are the defects that the QMS captured. We may not have prevented the defect being created, but containment systems prevented their release. Generally, these are captured in the system and addressed as nonconformances or deviations. While some would argue these events are caused by a range of reasons—including the catch all category of "human error"—generally they happen due to poor or suboptimal design of the manufacturing system.

Finally, at the very base of the iceberg are the events that never become significant issues at all. They are happening many times a day in virtually every organization: the batch record incorrectly filled in but corrected in time, the bottle placed in the wrong location but then moved. Corners cut to meet a deadline, the failure to document something as it "probably doesn't really matter."

The iceberg model stresses that to reduce the number and impact of more critical events above the water, one needs to address the drivers of these events further below the surface.

Systems thinking as applied to quality has parallels with the safety industry which pioneered many of these approaches. Accidents happen not because individuals are clumsy but because of an inherent failure of the system. To address this system failure, one needs to implement a safe system of work. It is worth revisiting this approach with respect to its relevance to quality.

A safety culture is based on four key drivers: an informed culture, a reporting culture, a learning culture, and finally a culture that is just [27]. You could argue that sustaining a culture of quality, as opposed to a safety-focused culture, one would rely on these same four factors.

Individuals need to be informed of how their contribution impacts quality and the impact of poor quality on the end user. There should be a culture where quality issues can be raised without fear of reprisal. The culture needs to be one where the talent of everybody can be applied for best results. Finally, the culture needs to be one where there is a large degree of trust and individuals can work in a collaborative fashion to advance a collective and clear understanding of the importance of quality.

Clearly, implementing any actions that support these four factors can only be beneficial in addressing underlying causes.

Unintended Consequences

The generation of unintended consequences arising from seemingly logical targets has been termed the Cobra effect. The term originated from the concern during British rule of India in the 1800s of the number of snake attacks taking place. Subsequently, the authorities offered a bounty for every dead cobra handed in. This reward encouraged some to breed the snakes to obtain the reward. On realizing this practice, the authorities immediately abandoned the practice of paying for dead snakes. Left with snakes they were unable to sell, breeders simply released them into the wild, resulting in an explosion in the snake population, an outcome completely opposite to the one originally intended.

An absolute focus on metrics can drive the wrong behaviors, sometimes with unintended consequences. One much publicized example is the UK government's four-hour accident and emergency (A&E) target it set in 2000. With creditable intentions to improve patient care, a maximum of four hours was set between a patient arriving at a hospital emergency department and either admission, transfer to another department, or discharge from the hospital. Attempts to meet this target were widely abused by several hospitals as they implemented creative ways to meet the target, which had no positive impact on patient care [28]. Despite over £820M being spent on A&E departments between 1998 and 2007, it was concluded that the four-hour target had no impact on overall patient care [29].

The above may appear to be extreme examples of essentially gaming the system, however they are worthy of review for all organizations that are focused on a metric-driven culture.

Even in the context of modern manufacturing, targets as well intentioned as production volume can encourage a focus on delivery at the detriment of other activities that are required for long-term success, such as maintenance and servicing. Even within the QMS, targets such as mean time to close a customer complaint or nonconformance numbers per area can drive the incorrect behaviors. Complaints are closed prematurely with the customer still dissatisfied or nonconformances underreported. Never underestimate the ingenuity of individuals and functions to play the system, especially when delivery against targets is linked to benefits, remuneration, and their own career progression.

Conversely, a business devoid of targets is simply unrealistic. Importantly, the outcome you are striving for needs to be clear and as covered in a previous chapter, linked to something the customer sees as valuable.

In summary, key to taking a systems approach to quality is the ability to peel back the different layers that are contributing to poor quality and be very careful how you attempt to change any of the elements that you expose.

One specific example we have already touched on that shows how the QMS behaves as a system under stress is any Quality leader's worst nightmare, a product recall. It is worth exploring this example further.

A Product Recall

While differing in the fine detail, all healthcare companies have recall management systems that are broadly similar. The issue is usually instigated by some form of internal finding, customer complaint, or pattern of complaints, which are then captured and investigated to determine whether they warrant further investigation. Sometimes these events meet the requirement of a reportable event to the regulatory bodies, and in more serious circumstances a recall or market withdrawal is needed.

This typically involves a process of escalation from the initial complaint, often up through the management layers up to the management board and the representative on the board ultimately, with the accountability and responsibility for quality and regulatory compliance. As such it would be expected that the whole process is simple, transparent, highly effective, and efficient in acting. This is not always the case.

The process of escalating the complaint involves multiple touchpoints with other parts of the QMS. In addition, it involves a host of other functions either providing data, expertise, or tasked with an activity to complete, often under very strict time constraints. Each are often responsible for their own processes, workload, priorities, and data siloes.

Despite the many interactions within this system—ones that even in a simple line diagram would become overly intricate—the system can be quantified. Metrics can be set for mean cycle time of the process, dwell time for investigations, the assessment of patient risk quantified, and a model of the system performance built if needed.

This only explains one aspect of the process, the one inhabiting the quantifiable world. However, this process also lives in another world; one which is not as easy to measure: the qualitative world. This is the world of opinions, feelings, and politics. It has a huge impact on how the system flows. It is the landscape of culture.

In this landscape even the purpose of the system becomes subjective, depending on the perspective of the individual. At a macroscopic level, the process has to meet a legal obligation, at a business level it is to protect the patient and understand and learn from failures. At the microscopic level—where the real work happens—individuals may be disenfranchised from such ideals, and be more concerned with workload, effort, and how they will be judged by the superiors.

Overlaid on to the process, as anybody having played a role in it will vouch, will be a highly political dimension. Individuals brief their managers on progress, who in turn brief senior managers, who brief their superiors. In the world of career politics, as much time is spent on communication flows as to addressing the actual matter in hand. Resources get sucked in, as the urgency increases, and functional boundaries break in the heat of firefighting. Senior managers offer personal perspectives of the best investigational strategy or what they feel is the cause of the issue. In the heat of a recall battle, everybody can suddenly become an expert.

During such high-profile events, often under the scrutiny of external forces such as the media, primal instincts and feelings take hold. The QMS comes under huge stress.

We challenge anyone who thinks that organizations and processes act as machines to live in the daily cauldron of a recall investigation. They will appreciate that the qualitative world of feelings and opinions is often more powerful than metrics and logic.

At such times the business and the QMS acts not just as a system, but one known as a complex adaptive system (CAS). Shortly, we will look at the QMS as an adaptive system in the next chapter and what it means for the management of quality. But first here are some practical aspects around how a systems approach can be applied to the management of quality.

Look at the Whole, Act on the Whole

You need to see the QMS not as separate processes, but as a whole. In practice it is useful to divide the QMS into constituent parts for ease of analysis, but always have a clear understanding that parts of the QMS are connected, some more than others. The Holy Trinity of the quality system: nonconformance, CAPA, and change control are obviously connected, and an increase in one flows work into the others.

This does pose practical challenges as the subsystems compete for the same resources, skill sets, and time. Your role as a leader is to be aware of this and to understand that however much you want to focus on the QMS, especially prior to regulatory inspection, resources always have other competing priorities and day jobs, especially when they work outside of the Quality organization.

It is key that you get alignment from your peer leaders whether that is at the executive board, management, or tactical level. You need to speak with one voice and act in unison with respect to quality. While Quality as a function may implement and oversee the QMS, functions outside of Quality make it work, and have huge influence in not allowing it to work at all.

A key process within the QMS to allow you to see the whole and act in a concerted manner is QSMR. Whether you perform this monthly, quarterly, or once a year, it is critical you make this process work for you. Here are some practical aspects to consider taking a systems approach.

Involve All Functions

The quality system crosses the whole of the business. If you just involve the Quality organization, it becomes very much a navel-gazing exercise. At best you are not getting other perspectives and a worst undermining the whole process.

Most quality system reviews involve the usual suspects in attendance such as Operations and R&D, but other functions need the opportunity to attend, contribute, and understand the quality system. How many reviews have Human Resources, Finance, information technology (IT), or Marketing in attendance? These functions have a huge role in how the organization performs and whether the QMS is satisfying all its customers' needs. Involve any function you think has a role to play in delivering this goal.

Explain the Power the Group Has

You will need to do more than just explain the purpose of the meeting from a regulatory perspective. You will need to articulate the power the meeting has to shape the QMS and determine whether it is doing its job for the business.

You need to explain why attendees are there, the contribution they need to make, and the importance of agreeing the allocation of resources to address identified issues or opportunities.

Create a Dialogue and Decide

In essence, QSMR is reviewing data that supports whether all aspects of the quality system are meeting customer needs. Each area needs a clear conclusion of whether the data supports a well-functioning system. QSMR should not be death by PowerPoint. It should be focusing on areas that need help and not focus on areas that are in control.

Sadly, many organizations do not want to put negative data in presentations that would indicate to an auditor they have an area that needs improvement. This defeats the main purpose of the meeting. Sure, an auditor will focus on any red metrics, but you just need to explain in the documentation what you are doing to address any shortfall or why action is not needed.

This will involve having an active conversation about what the data is telling you. There should be differences of opinion as you move toward consensus. QSMR is something you are part of, rather than something you have done to you.

Document It Well

QSMR is your window into the quality system. It is also a window for how internal agencies will view your QMS. These documents, however well they are presented, will be closely reviewed by others. Review them closely through their eyes. Do they tell an adequate story? Are they clear? Does the data support your conclusions? What actions are you prioritizing?

Is This a Problem or Symptom?

It is human nature, when presented with an issue, to jump to the conclusion of what the problem is and what the solution should be. This is an innate behavior hardwired through thousands of years of evolution to keep us alive. While not every situation warrants a period of quiet reflection—if your clothes are on fire you need to act now; most day-to-day situations aren't life threatening or require such urgency.

Things to consider include questioning whether the presentation of the issue is the real problem, or are there more foundational causes hiding below the waterline you need to understand and address? Conversely, if the solution is blatantly obvious and the issue is critical, you need to act. Don't get wrapped up in the methodology unduly. Sometimes getting a fix in quickly, one that just works is more important. If needed, perform multiple rounds of root cause investigation and action.

Try and Understand

You will need to understand the problem, and this will involve asking questions. Questions you don't know the answers to. Not to validate your own views but to truly comprehend. Is this view an opinion or fact? Can it be verified independently? Conversely, you don't want to go overboard and appear to interrogate people.

As we will cover further, in organizations, opinions are as powerful—even more so—than facts. You can verify a fact. It is hard to refute an opinion or belief.

"There are two beers in my fridge" versus "I have enough beer in my fridge."

The first statement you can measure the veracity of. The second statement is a relative position depending on your view of beer as a beverage.

To improve your understanding, some questions to ask are: How do they see it from their perspective? Why do they have this viewpoint? Why are they saying this?

It is more difficult to understand certain issues as a leader, not because you are intellectually less capable, but simply because information is filtered before you get it. In all organizations, however flat the management structure and how approachable you feel you are, your opinion as a leader will matter to everybody. This makes understanding what people truly feel, rather than them telling you what they think you want to hear, very difficult.

Individuals may not be as open and honest with you as you would like. As an aside, events where senior management meet with staff over tea and sandwiches rarely works from the staff's perspective, but do make senior leaders feel they are connecting with the organization. Here are more practical ways of gaining a better understanding.

Walk and Talk

One of best ways to get to know somebody is to share a car journey with them. This is often successful as it is a neutral venue. In addition, there is no pressure for conversation between the periods of silence, as you both watch the world go by. Both parties can reflect on what has been said and decide or not to explore a topic further, or just remain silent. Soon an unpressured dialogue often begins to take place. While taking individuals for a spin around the block in your car is impractical, there are aspects that can be replicated by walking together either around the building, outside, or between locations. People will generally be more open and more able to offer unguarded views when in is wrapped up in some other activity. At the worst if you don't learn anything new, you will both get a bit of exercise.

Lighten Up

As a leader, you can't expect people to open up if you don't take a broader interest in what motivates them. While some may be less comfortable talking about family and their personal life, everybody likes to feel that they are being noticed and tangential subjects such as "how long they been with the company, current role?" and so on, are useful ways to open up a dialogue.

There is a catch, however. You cannot expect people to open up unless you share a little of yourself. You will be pleasantly surprised how interested people will be and the unwritten contract is they will often reveal something of themselves. If as a leader you feel this is too difficult, we would question whether you are a leader or just feel you are. You are doing this as you need to understand their viewpoint and unless you do this you cannot help them or your organization.

Does This Matter?

If you conclude an issue is a real problem, it helps if you take a step back and ask yourself does it really matter? You can only answer this question if you put yourself in the customer's shoes. As we have covered previously, there are potentially many different customers you will need to consider. In addition, by satisfying one customer are you dissatisfying another? Conversely you may need to implement changes in one area that may have little benefit, or even have a detrimental impact on this system, but need to be implemented for the greater good of the organization or another process. Your job as a quality leader is to articulate this bigger picture view.

Look for Patterns

When you take a systems approach you are looking for patterns in the data that may not tell you much in isolation, but may give you an indication of a more systemic issue. For example, are errors or defects across the subsystems driven by patterns that may be related to ineffective training. Is there commonality? Are patterns related to seasons linked to staff turnover or end of year or financial year deadlines? The individual data points may not be telling you much, but your challenge as a leader is to connect the dots.

Wait for Results

We live in an age of instant gratification, where reward is immediate. This culture also pervades business where it is hoped that a change of personnel or process will create instant success.

This isn't what happens in a system view of an organization. Actions take time to take effect. With the interconnected nature of systems, it may take time for the impact of changes to work through all the subsystems. The best you can do as a leader is to explain this upfront. This is especially true regarding the timescales for any transformative activity that you are rolling out in the medium to longer timeframe. Of course, everybody wants the low hanging fruit quickly, but that isn't necessarily where the juiciest apples are.

In summary, systems thinking has changed how organizations view themselves and the world around them. While interconnected systems thinking assumes a degree of cause and effect between one system and another, the link may be complicated. The challenge for a system view of the world is that it has failed to result in organizations that are completely predictable as we would have hoped for, especially under the medium-to-longer timeframe. This has led to additional approaches to understanding the real world involving models that can see the world as having a more changing and adaptive behavior, which we will explore in the next chapter and how it relates to the QMS.

Summary

The QMS is a quality management *system*.

- Treat the quality system as a system and not a collection of isolated processes.
- Do not expect to influence one part of the system without perturbing another.
- Try to truly understand the system before acting. Look for underlying causes.
- Beware of the unintended consequences of your actions.

CHAPTER 6

Worldviews and the QMS

Complexity

The Reality of Life

One of the foundations of either process- or systems-driven thinking— is the presumption of cause and effect. Every effect has some underlying cause or causes, and the relationship may be complicated and require us to experiment to understand the relationship. With enough effort, it can be understood, and the performance of the system predicted. The root cause or contributing causes can be identified, be they defective units of production, delays in manufacturing, customer dissatisfaction, noncompliance against procedures, or even product recalls. We will typically approach such challenges with this reductionistic mindset. No system is so complicated it cannot be taken apart and understood.

But the world isn't like that, is it? As individuals we do unpredictable things, organizations do unpredictable things. Despite all your best efforts to bring your business and organization under your control, it is probably fair to say a large portion of your day is comprised of firefighting and resolving issues that you didn't expect to happen. Even taking a systems approach, though a huge step forward, has the presumption that the complete system can be explained and predicted, though clearly at times it cannot. There is a conflict between the world of management in all its forms (be it quality, supply chain, distribution, etc.) and the messy reality of the real world. It is a world that is constantly changing and almost impossible to control. So where did this management expectation that we can control the world even come from? Surprisingly, from the world of physics.

Forces, Thermodynamics, and Management

In essence, there are two opposing views of the world. At one extreme is the world of order. It is a world that Isaac Newton described to explain the motion of bodies such as planets and the forces that act on them. Newton's laws of motion describe the movement of everything from billiard balls to whole planets. It covers a world of inputs that can be controlled and outputs that can be verified. It is a world of predictability and order. It also forms the very basis of modern management thinking we know today, the basis of machine thinking, and a reductionistic view of the world. It has shaped how individuals, organizations, and even governments behave.

At the other extreme is a world devoid of order. It is a world where everything becomes more random, eventually moving to a thermodynamic equilibrium. This world translated into one that resonated with the field of economics. It is one of market forces, supply and demand. In truth, the real world sits at neither of these extremes. It behaves neither completely like a machine nor is it completely disordered. Despite this, we often treat the world as if it were at the poles of opposing behavior. Between the two extremes sits the world of complexity.

It's a Complex World Out There

We are surrounded by complex systems. Many we take for granted. They are large and small. The natural world has an abundance of them, from flocks of birds to whole ecosystems. We accept them for what they are and do not question their presence. You are reading and understanding the words on this page through the ability of one of the most unique examples of a complex system: your brain.

But when we look at our organizations and lives, we want the world to be different to what it really is. We want it to be predictable, ordered, and stable. By their nature, complex systems are none of these things.

In *Embracing Complexity*, Jean Boulton and others cover the attributes of complex systems [30]. These can be summarized as follows:

- **Systemic**: Processes are interconnected, but the relationship between them may not always be linear. A small change in one process may have a significant impact in another. There is synergy. You cannot understand the system until you look at it as a whole.

- **Multiscalar**: Understanding a complex system can only be achieved if we look at it at different levels. The behaviors of the individual, group, or collective within the system may be very different.

- **Diverse**: Changes in the system and internal or external pressure results in adaptability. As the system grows, specialisms result in niche areas that may exploit the environment.

- **Contingent**: The future is path dependent and shaped by context and history: Complex systems behave as they do because of both their past and current state. This shapes how they will behave now and in the future.

- **Episodic change**: The system may be resilient to change, or it may tip into new forms. The change can occur in fits and starts. There is more than one future. The future is neither predetermined, nor happens through chance. The system can change through self-organization. Patterns can emerge. These patterns may be good or bad.

An analogy is a car. A mechanical car key of a vehicle over 20 years old could be considered a simple device. Though a modern car, with its electronic systems it could be considered complicated. Importantly, the relationship between cause and effect is understandable. For example, the car slows when the brake pedal is pressed. Braking does not cause the radio to operate or the windows to open. Where the cause-and-effect relationship cannot always be predicted, and the system is constantly changing, it can be defined as a "complex." The movement of traffic on a freeway can be considered complex, where even small changes in speed at the head of a line of traffic can have a significant impact further behind. It is not possible to fully understand or predict behavior, even if you are able to see the complete system as a whole. How often have you been stuck in traffic without an apparent cause, for the holdup to then suddenly disappear?

Complexity, a Framework for Decision Making

David Snowden in the late 1990s built on the concept of complexity and developed a framework as a way of understanding the world based on different viewpoints [31]. He termed it the Cynefin framework, Cynefin being the Welsh word for habitat. The framework forms a basis for how decisions can be made, contingent on the specific scenario in question.

In his framework, the ordered world—described on the right-hand side of Figure 6.1, is split into either the Clear or Complicated. In the former domain, the link between cause and effect is very easy to understand and obvious. While for a complicated system the relationship still holds, but needs expertise, or testing to fully understand.

The left-hand side includes domains where the world is less ordered. It is split into either a domain described as Complex, where the relationship

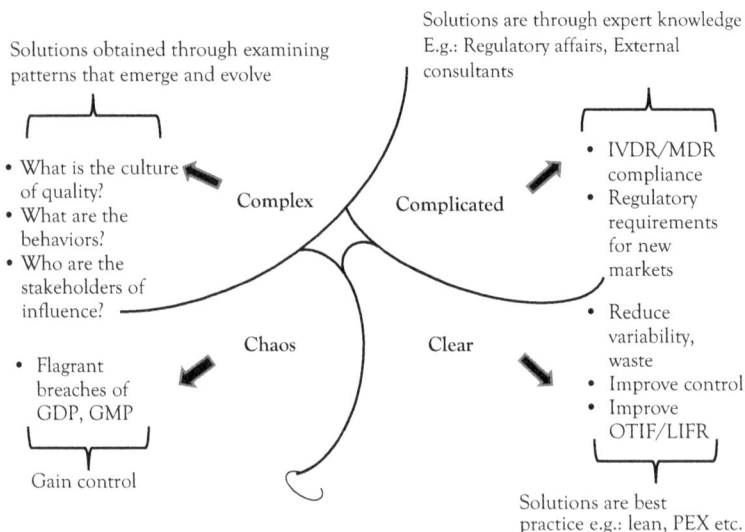

Figure 6.1 The Cynefin framework and the management of quality

Source: https://cynefin.io/wiki/Cynefin. Reproduced by permission.

between cause and effect doesn't always hold, or changes, and finally a region that describes a Chaotic world.

Snowden split the world into four regions not so much as a tool to categorize, but as a framework to demonstrate how even in the same scenario, multiple viewpoints worlds are often presented simultaneously. More importantly, decisions in each region can be very different but equally appropriate. Such a framework has been given the support of bodies such as the European Union to foster better decision making [32].

For issues presenting themselves in the Clear domain, the solution is usually obvious: implement best practice. There is no need to do anything further and certainly no reason to reinvent the wheel if the best solution is already on offer.

When situations aren't so simple, but a bit more Complicated, then several correct answers are equally valid once the situation is better understood through either expert knowledge or experimentation. In a world of the Complicated, expertise is often needed to fully understand what is going on, be it engineering, business, or similar specialisms, but there may be many ways of solving the same problem.

The relationship between cause and effect in the Complex domain can be changing or not hold at all. In this domain often the best solution is to observe. The relationship between cause and effect can only be recognized with hindsight. In this domain, attempting to understand through experimentation often fails. The sheer process of acting often impacts the system in ways that cannot be predicted. Finally, in the domain of Chaos, picking any solution is better than nothing. The leader just needs to act.

The Cynefin Framework and the Management of Quality

Any organization on a journey to transform its quality system will face several challenges. These may be short- or medium term and of low or more urgent priority. It is worth looking at change through the eyes of the framework described previously. While all organizations may be in different places on this journey, the following are a few examples of things to be considered for each of the domains, as shown in Figure 6.1.

Any business that is struggling with product variability, waste, and challenges with supplying the customer has several off-the-shelf methodologies that have been around for decades. While these improvement techniques are powerful, alone they are not enough. Sadly today, not every business has become efficient and effective after many years of applying such approaches. Even companies that pioneered such methodology have not been without their own challenges over recent years.

Issues that present themselves in the Complicated domain include new and more stringent regulations, standards, and often-increasing expectations of regulatory bodies around the world. These expectations are often highly detailed and complicated. They need expert opinion to translate requirements into activities you can implement to meet them. These issues are often solved through the use of experts with intimate and specific knowledge not available to you.

Issues that sit in the Complex domain are the meat of this book. They cover aspects such as the culture of quality in your organization, the stakeholders you need to influence and the behaviors you want to encourage.

Finally, issues about quality that present themselves in the Chaotic domain are items that need addressing swiftly. For example, flagrant breaches of GMP and associated documentation need addressing head on and quickly. Likewise, any sudden breaches in your quality control processes need reacting to immediately. In this domain, it is not a time for reflection and some hard calls will have to be made based on incomplete information.

The above guidance is not all encompassing but hopefully demonstrates the power of the framework. It helps you as a leader to ask yourself in any given scenario: Which domain(s) am I in? What is the most appropriate action(s)?

The most difficult domain to live in is obviously the Complex domain. This domain infers that you as a leader may not be as in control as you may want. This aspect is worth exploring a little more.

Complexity and Being Not Fully in Control

Phillip Streatfield—a quality control manager within a large multinational—explored how much this control is real or at times just an illusion in his book *The Paradox of Control in Organizations* [33]. His work is revealing as it gives a perspective, and one you would not expect from an individual in a function where quality and control is the very essence of the position. Experiencing the organization at a time of huge flux—the business was going through a merger—he asks the valid question "who is in control?" and explores several themes including the formation of dynamic patterns, self-organization, and emergence.

He concludes that even when we may appear in control, there is enough wiggle in the system to cause change to happen. Even for processes you would expect to be tightly controlled such as pharmaceutical production where he worked. He concluded that in real life, management at times appears to be making it up as they go along.

Streatfield offered the advice that as managers "we have to find the courage to carry on participating creatively in the construction of new meaning in spite of not knowing." Managers are in a paradoxical position where they are both in control and not in control simultaneously. This itself can cause huge angst and Streatfield states:

> For me, management has come to mean living with both sides of the control paradox at the same time. This means acting on the basis of an expectation of an outcome, knowing full well that it is unlikely to materialize, requiring me to be ready to handle the consequences whatever they may be. It involves developing effective ways of handling the anxiety of "not knowing." Streatfield 2001 [33]

His views may appear at times heretical in the context of a modern manufacturing plant but are well observed and valid. Streatfield's view of an organization as a complex responsive process echoes much of the literature about how complex systems behave from the standpoint of one who is fully aware of the paradox of his own views.

If you are a leader who wants to be in complete control, then any model that suggests that this may not be even possible, could be very difficult to deal with. Potentially it could lead to frustration and stress. Conversely, acknowledging that you live in a slightly uncontrollable world can be refreshing. In addition, variability and change leads to innovation and agility and has its upside.

Being able to live with uncertainty may not be a natural attribute for a quality professional, but is a key competency to deal with the uncertainties of real life in the role. It does, however, require a different mindset to one traditionally found within the quality profession.

The Quality System as a Complex Adaptive System

Let us revisit the QMS in the context of some of the attributes of complex systems.

Systemic

The processes within the QMS are connected. For example, poor design of products and manufacturing systems can result in surges in nonconformances post launch of a new product. Weak or inadequate supplier controls can result in the generation of defects and audit deficiencies. Inadequate staff training can result in nonconformances, scrap, and potentially, customer complaints. Errors in documentation can have no impact, or in the case of specifications, huge repercussions on the quality of products manufactured and direct impact on patient safety. All parts of the QMS are interlinked and even small changes, or more often, lack of focus in one area, can have repercussions on other parts of the system.

Multiscalar

The QMS operates on many levels. Looking at complaint handling, not every call a customer makes to the business is necessarily a complaint, some are just enquiries about product use or delivery. Some communications are potential complaints that is, allegations that the product or service is not meeting their expectation. A proportion of these may be valid, and spawn investigations into product quality and a further subset may constitute issues that warrant recall or market withdrawal of the product. While logged as individual complaints in the system, not all complaints are the same. This scalar nature can also be seen with documentation.

Most organizations have some form of document hierarchy. At the top usually sits the Quality Policy (QP), which sets out the quality intent and direction of the organization, usually in a single document. Below it usually sits a Quality Manual, which sets out in more detail the quality expectations of each area at a very high level. Below this sits Policies for each QMS area, with more granularity on what is needed. Below these sit Procedures that describe how the intent for each respective area can be met in practice, which are then detailed more in the form of Work Instructions. Below these sit the Forms that are completed during QMS execution as documentary evidence that the intent is being met in line with the policies.

The QMS operates at multiple levels simultaneously. It is an essential aspect of its behavior.

Diverse

Complex systems have variety. This does not necessarily mean this is good or bad. It just happens.

The history of quality management within a single organization is itself a story of evolution. If an organization is small then a single individual may have to wear many quality hats: design, supplier, compliance, regulatory affairs, and so on. As the business grows—and in line with how quality management has evolved—specialisms begin to evolve—and to an extent self-organize, another feature of complex systems—each accountable for a specific area of the QMS.

This specialization has several pros and cons. The main advantages include specialization to support defined needs and requirements. Regulatory affairs is a specialism. Regulations across countries and regions are complicated and the consequences of not understanding them or not meeting their requirements are significant. Other areas within the QMS also evolve over time to cover specific areas: suppliers, document control, and so on.

The disadvantage of specialism is that the subfunctions become siloed, unable to flex. Their ability to support the business outside their specific areas of competency becomes lost. This specialization is often confusing to stakeholders in the business who may not appreciate the specific accountabilities within the Quality unit.

For example, in a medium-sized operational plant of around 350 to 400 individuals, it would not be unusual for around 50 individuals to be part of the Quality function. Despite such numbers, the number of individuals able to make quality decisions required to support day-to-day operations often resides with only a few individuals within functions such as Quality Operations or Quality Engineering, and often restricted to the management layer. Even within these subfunctions, the decision making is sometimes inconsistent and restricted to those with experience, ability, and confidence to make risk-based objective decisions. Specialism can come at a cost. Variety and evolution do not always result in optimum endpoints in nature or in business systems. The balance between specialism and a generalist approach is often a tricky one.

As Streatfield found, it is virtually impossible to remove all "wiggle" in the system and eliminate all variation. A good example is the CAPA process.

One would expect that organizations that have long-standing and mature CAPA systems should have eliminated all nonconformances over time and eventually driven them to zero. This is not the reality. The system that can almost appear infinite in the ways it can create deviations and new ways to nonconform. In many respects, it may be a fruitless task implementing CAPA for a special cause issue that by its pure randomness may never happen again. Often, the nonconformance system appears like a bag of numbered balls from which you pick out a selection each month, react to them, but become frustrated when you appear never to empty the bag. This is the very nature of a complex system. It is impossible to pin down and gain complete control.

Contingent

Most businesses have a past and come with a degree of baggage that shapes their current state and influences their future paths. The QMS is no different. A host of factors will have shaped your current structure. These include the technology that the QMS hangs off; the legacy of audits; past leader's worldviews; the level of risk tolerance; and the background experience of those that are currently part of the Quality organization.

At a macrolevel, every QMS has a history. It may even have multiple origins if you integrate different companies. At a microlevel the same is true.

Documentation is also often shaped by the past. Islands of very specific direction sit within a sea of general guidance, the former the result of audit responses or CAPA bolted on to documentation and procedures.

Often, quality systems become hostages to such updates, as past modifications are protected from change. Accepting that the past should not hamstring the future can be a huge obstacle for many quality systems. Eventually, the QMS may eventually collapse under its own weight, unable to adapt, or simply exist. The challenge is to know when to prune back and when to leave alone. Conversely, when areas do need obvious improvement, one size does not always fit all with respect to QMS improvements. What may have worked successfully within one organization may be very detrimental to another.

Episodic Change

One aspect of complex systems is how they respond to external stimuli. They may stay relatively unchanged for long periods, then go through a phase of rapid transformation as the system reaches a tipping point and the system is driven toward a new equilibrium. Several factors can increase the potential for this tipping point to occur. These can be broadly grouped into external and internal factors.

If we look at these factors from the vantage point of the QMS, external factors include new regulations; a more competitive business environment resulting in the cost of quality being less tolerated from a financial perspective, and greater customer expectations of quality of products and services. In addition, another external factor that acts as a huge catalyst for episodic change is technology.

Internal forces driving rapid change include increasing expectations of business partners within organizations on the role and value of the Quality function. It is becoming less tolerated that Quality is just a "necessary evil" that businesses must put up with. There is a growing expectation that Quality should provide insight into current and future customer needs. Internal forces driving episodic change also include new leadership of the Quality function—often through appointments specifically tasked with driving change—but also pressure from executive boards that the Quality organization aligns, supports and actively contributes with the direction the enterprise is heading.

When viewed through the lens of complexity, QMSs do really behave as complex systems. While this may be regarded as a new concept, the view of the QMS as a specific type of complex system that is, a CAS has been expressed by many [34–36].

Several authors have noted that the QMS does sit in a unique position. It exists in the world of control, exemplified by the Newtonian paradigm of how we understand the world and resultant views on process control that stem from such a view. It is the machine perspective. It also exists in a world with all the behaviors of a complex, exploratory, and learning world. The QMS has feet planted in both worlds and needs to be treated as such.

Importantly, if we allow a system to decay to equilibrium, there can be no further change. Conversely, if we attempt to restrain the world and transposing a machine view on reality, it may not work. At best, we solidify the system or at worst, get frustrated attempting to restrain the unrestrainable.

The consequence of this is tension. Others have noted that the essential conflict between equilibrium and change, control and innovation.

> The bottom line is: one must manage systems to be in control and out of control at the same time. Dooley [34]

What does this mean for the QMS and the ability to design and implement more effective systems? Attributes of complex systems may appear nebulous and difficult to translate into the real world, especially the world of quality management, standards, and regulations.

Jean Boulton and others describe complex systems as exhibiting five attributes [30]. While others have viewed such systems as being akin to biological entities with a range of properties [36].

While these views have validity, the QMS differs from a true CAS in one key respect that is, its ability to self-direct. Generally, complex systems are not cognizant. An ecosystem or financial market has no self-awareness or ability to influence proactively its current or future state in ways that you as a leader can. More importantly such subcategorization of the QMS, while intellectually fulfilling, has little relevance for the business leader unless it leads to some practical use.

Treating the QMS as a CAS—or by extension the Quality organization itself—for it to be truly successful you must exploit four key aspects.

You need the ability to:

- Balance innovation and control
- Manage risk
- Model appropriate leadership
- Continually pursue improvement

Balance Innovation and Control

A key attribute of a successful QMS is to balance innovation and control to deliver products/services that meet or exceed expectations. This is inherently a challenge. The desire to achieve consistency during production, reduce product variability, and control the manufacturing system is laudable. For certain tasks within the QMS, for example adding the specific components that make up a formulation, you must have consistency and reproducibility, as a mistake can have a serious impact. Allowing variability is not an option. While designing, implementing, and maintaining electronic systems such as electronic batch records and bar coding is onerous, they do ensure that processes have a high degree of error-proofing.

Importantly, this need to control should not be translated into a requirement to drive homogeneity into the quality system and those responsible for it. There are downsides of attempting to highly constrain the QMS.

Increased control generally comes at a resource cost. Hardwiring aspects of the QMS, for example through electronic systems involves a cost that must be balanced against the benefit. Standardization for standardization's sake, especially across a business enterprise, may feel the purest approach, but is often not adding value for the customer.

In the eyes of the FDA, noncompliance with internal procedures indicates a weak or even nonfunctioning QMS, which equates in their eyes to noncompliance with federal law. Overly prescriptive or complex procedures become rich pickings for external auditors. Organizations can quickly struggle to comply with their own self-imposed and sometimes contradictory documentation. Clear, simple, and not overly prescriptive procedures are generally best. If the procedure is prescriptive, then the business will need to provide resources to comply with them. Again, control comes at a cost.

It is sometimes difficult to fight against the inherent desire of those in the Quality profession, who for valid reasons, attempt to impose control. The quality professional tends to be intolerant of outliers. While such an approach may work admirably for a manufacturing process, it is very easy—subconsciously or otherwise—to transfer such thinking to people. Obtaining consensus is no more than trying to average viewpoints and eliminating outlier opinion. Often outlier opinion has real value.

Diversity of opinion offers the potential for new ideas, innovation, and agility [36] and has been shown to be a positive attribute for an organization [37–38]. For quality professionals dealing with outlier opinion is far easier said than done, as often viewpoints are strongly held. Complexity theory has not taken hold in manufacturing organizations compared with other areas more aligned with the social sciences, as the concept is philosophically messy and untidy. It runs counter to machine-thinking that is at almost the foundation of total quality management (TQM). The world of complexity is not neat. But it is the way the real world behaves, whether we like it or not. To build better products that help more patients and support and grow the business, the modern quality professional may not totally embrace complexity but does need to recognize the concept and the alternative viewpoint.

It is possible with effort to force control onto the QMS, but the complex nature of the beast makes this at times a difficult and resource-hungry task. We would argue that the optimum position is a balance that ensures both compliance and flexibility, allowing the QMS to react, evolve, and change as the needs of the business change.

This balance can be seen as to how change is often managed in the quality system. At one extreme there are cloud-based applications. Change control can be hardwired with a workflow used to review and approve documentation changes. At the other extreme there can be a paper-based systems—or even complete absence of systems—which by their nature are highly flexible but prone to interpretation, errors, and require the documentation to be actively managed. There are obviously pros and cons around either approach. It can be argued the most optimum approach may be a hybrid model that offers consistency of an electronic workflow but offers flexibility of a paper-based approach. The response will be dependent on the specific circumstances of each organization.

Importantly, the most appropriate approach to managing Control versus Change is contingent on the situation. Quality management faces a continual tussle between these two elements. There are scenarios where Quality needs to be "hands-off" and take a step back. Often, in apparently chaotic circumstances the conditions for innovation thrives. For example, developing new business models or products often requires an environment of unconstrained thinking.

As the need for control increases, more structured approaches are needed. At the other extreme at the process level, when compliance and absolute control is required, approaches more based on lean and Six Sigma are best (see Figure 6.2).

The challenges you have as a Quality leader include being able to teach your organization to recognize different scenarios and understand which approach is best.

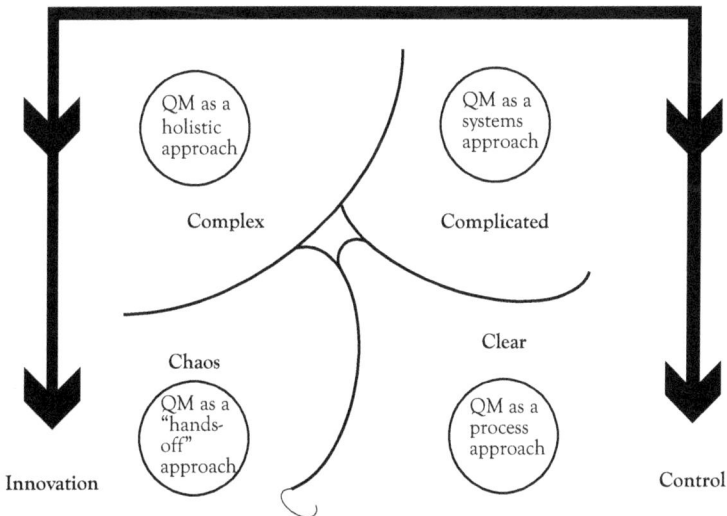

Figure 6.2 Management of quality contingent on scenario

Manage Risk

A key—if not the only function of a Quality leader—is to manage risk to deliver the best-balanced outcome for patient, customer, regulator, and stockholder. Easier said than done.

One of the misconceptions about Quality, even from those who work in the function, is that it is a world of black and white. Everything has a specification, and it is easy to separate good from bad. In truth, anybody who has worked in Quality soon realizes it is a world of uncertainty. It has many shades of gray, which require judgments to be made with often incomplete data, requiring risk to be assessed under conditions of sometimes total ambiguity. Creating environments that are highly controlled often stifles the ability of individuals to make these judgment calls, suppresses creativity and innovation, and often stops the ability to move quickly when needed.

While for some this may feel a more nebulous concept than is comfortable, there is one area that virtually all quality managers accept without question and is one that also sits between order and nonorder: statistical process control (SPC).

SPC is generally considered to be a rational tool that assumes objectivity and is used by every quality professional. Based on the methodology, judgments are made daily and products accepted or scrapped. But, by its very definition it is probabilistic in nature. It involves uncertainty and degrees of doubt. It sits between unpredictability and certainty. It attempts to often fit reality into a normal distribution. Often statistics is used to prove or disprove a hypothesis of what is good and what is bad, often casting aside the underlying degree of uncertainty that is inherent in the methodology. Ninety-five percent confidence really equates to a 1 in 20 chance your assessment could be wrong.

It is up to your organization to decide how much uncertainty you will tolerate. How much proof is needed before that product is released? Which is essentially the core role of the quality professional: dealing with uncertainty and managing risk. Importantly, the pragmatic quality professional understands the concept of special cause events and outliers. Things that don't behave as expected may be telling us something very important.

In essence, balancing risk is difficult. The QMS has many masters: compliance, business sustainability, and customer experience. Often metrics that assess the performance of separate processes within the QMS may conflict with respect to differing needs of each of the customers. The question should be: is the QMS good enough and adequately satisfying the needs of all its customers? Is it reducing risk for one customer at the expense of another? This requires the QMS to be viewed as a holistic entity and to balance risks appropriately.

Model Appropriate Leadership

With respect to the QMS, the quality system is more than a combination of its parts. This does have consequences for where you see the QMS residing; from a philosophical point of view that is, ownership is collective rather than residing within the Quality function or owned by the Vice President of Quality. It is a similar question of who ultimately owns and is responsible for the quality of the products a business makes and sells. Legal responsibility lies with the nominated person on the executive board, but in most mature organizations this is seen as a collective responsibility owned by all in the organization. For an effective QMS, the responsibility for quality should be shared. This needs to be actively explained to the organization. All individuals have a direct responsibility for quality and the quality system is not a system owned and executed solely by the Quality organization.

A key challenge for a leader in Quality is intrinsically linked to what you believe to be your purpose. The: why? As we will touch on this, there are a range of leadership approaches. While there may be times where you need to give explicit instruction, a servant leadership style often fits best with your need to ensure the QMS and the Quality organization serves the needs of its different customer groups [39].

That is not to say, you must please everybody all the time but develop a balanced approach. Step back from the detail and give direction with an approach that meets multiple needs. Importantly, articulate a vision of where your organization area is heading: What are the challenges? How will they be addressed?

While there are whole fields of business research on the best behaviors needed to drive change, what is clear is that those who are stuck in the weeds of tactical execution are not always best able to give clear direction. An individual may have excellent technical skills and be able to execute, but this emphasis on the detail can be a huge hinderance in a leadership position. Sadly, many individuals who are better placed to act as exemplary individual contributors are often put in positions where they need to take a bigger picture view and are unable to do so. Beware, if your QMS is overly complicated, awash with clauses and details, then appointing leaders who are very conversant with this level of minutiae may simply perpetuate or increase this state of affairs.

In essence, maintaining a highly prescriptive QMS can create leaders who are born from such a system. These leaders may not be suited to leading the business effectively.

One important challenge is to not only see the Quality organization as it is today, but how it could be in the future. It is a challenge that warrants its own chapter. As the QMS grows, it becomes harder to control and the challenge of continual improvement becomes harder but improve it must.

Additionally, while you as a leader must give direction, control must happen from the bottom, or where the work is done—the Gemba. This is where the work that impacts quality really happens. Control cannot be applied from the top. True quality cannot be inspected into a product. It must come from the design and production systems based on the voice of customer who will use the products. This applies as much to the sub-processes of the QMS as to the end products.

Businesses that have a top down—command and control—approach are inefficient, ineffective, and unsustainable. Eventually, senior managers become bottlenecks in the decision-making process or make poor decisions based on inaccurate perceptions of reality. Again, it is about relinquishing a level of control for the greater good. The role of the servant leader is to enable the organization to think for itself and most importantly to improve and grow.

Continually Pursue Improvement

Despite its complex behavior, the quality system is not some nebulous entity that is impossible to change, and we should give up. Quite the opposite, improvements can be made. Learning a new language or skill requires practice and success generally builds more success. Improving the

QMS is no different. Successes should form the foundation for further advances, but these returns must be cultivated. They do not happen without planning, effort, and action to reinforce advances made. An organization that sees continual improvement as an essential and ongoing activity is better placed than one that is wrapped up in the specific methodology on how this can be achieved.

All successful organizations seek new ways and approaches to learn and improve. Importantly, they build on advances already delivered. Your change effort will be blown off course at times. Your job as a leader is to make sure it is heading in the right direction for all your customers.

Much of continuous improvement over recent years has been focused on understanding the cause of defects, removing them, and preventing them from happening again. Underlying this is the desire to move toward greater and greater consistency and predictability. This is laudable but often does not foster new approaches.

For a complex adaptive QMS to be successful there needs to be a degree of experimentation to trial new ideas, with the understanding that most new ways of doing things will often result in failure.

This is difficult. Organizations don't like things that fail. Individuals don't like being associated with approaches that fail. But piloting, trialing, and experimenting is part of moving forward. We are so afraid of failure that when we do try new ways, we also shy away from calling it what it is when it doesn't hit the spot.

One of the faults in some uses of continuous improvement methodology today, is that it often cannot be seen to fail. By their very definition, endeavors are successes before they start. A continuous improvement initiative, when presented back to senior managers, is rarely showcased as a failure.

The consequence of this is important. Ideas that are poor, weak, or deliver far below the mark, are given credibility far above their worth. All because we are too afraid of embracing failure. For the modern quality professional this must stop. We should encourage new approaches and, despite appropriate risk assessment, expect many to fail, but we need to be honest and constructive in our assessment. Above all, do not let this stifle experimentation. Evaluate the results realistically and learn from them.

Sometimes a planned approach does not reveal the best way forward. Øgland noted his puzzlement in implementing a QMS transformation at "the apparent failure of the highly structured and management driven development method" and the rapid success of the "'make-it-up-as-you-go-along' approach" [21]. Sometimes approaches that were never planned can open new ways of thinking.

As we have seen there is an essential conflict between equilibrium and change, control and innovation, and the need to balance stability and movement. Keeping the system at a point of disequilibrium in many ways supports creativity [21, 36].

It is in this world that the quality professional operates: a world perpetually at disequilibrium. This is the essence of the role of the quality professional. It is neither Quality Control nor Quality Assurance but Quality Leadership. For those in the quality profession who struggle with the concepts of systems, complexity, and uncertainty, we'd say that nothing presented is new. It is just the reality of our business, organizations, and society today.

The QMS isn't some uncontrollable entity you cannot influence. Greater risk can be accepted or rejected. The balance between all the customers of the QMS can be adjusted based on needs and changes in environment. You as a leader have the power to influence this. You need to leave no stone unturned in the continual pursuit of data-driven prioritized improvements to satisfy all the customers of the QMS.

Summary

The world can operate at multiple levels, often simultaneously. Being able to recognize these and responding appropriately is the key to success. At times Quality needs to take a step back, at other times observe or experiment to understand. Certain situations require Quality to enforce control.

- As a complex adaptive system, a quality system can be unpredictable and changing. The comfort blanket of cause-and-effect may not be available.
- Understand the system by observation.

- You are striving to gain clarity rather than achieve certainty.
- Be able to differentiate the clear, complicated, complex, and the chaotic.
- Make your decision making contingent on the presentation of events.
- Deciding not to act can still be the correct decision.
- Use the customer as your reference point for all decision making.

CHAPTER 7

Organization

Differing Voices

If you are going to drive the transformation of a Quality organization and implement some of the approaches described in the previous chapters, you're going to have to face how the organization should best be structured. The purpose of this chapter is not an esoteric discussion on organizational optimization or how the workplace will evolve in the coming years. The prime purpose of this book is to help you implement changes now, lay the ground for changes to come, and better prepare your QMS for future events.

How you organize your Quality organization will depend essentially on who you ask. There are many stakeholders with vested interests and opinions on this matter. These include those in the continuous improvement industry, your business partners, and the traditional brands of Quality that have arisen from the TQM movement.

The question you will have as a leader, in this clarion call of differing voices, who should you listen to? In fact, why should you pay heed to the opinions within this book?

In our defense, we would argue the following. While the authors have certification in both applying lean and Six Sigma, we have learnt firsthand not only the benefits but also the pitfalls of applying such methodology in Quality organizations. They have substantial merit, but at times, they can prevent other approaches from taking hold or even being considered. The authors have attempted to distil some of the newer approaches that we feel help plug some of the gaps.

In this chapter, we articulate approaches that we have found to work well. More importantly, these are approaches that have been applied in the real world. They cover not only the transformation of a Quality organization within multinational healthcare corporations, but also the learnings and experience from moving a Quality organization from a multinational corporate entity to a standalone organization during a multiyear carveout exercise. This is experience that has been acquired the hard way, applying them in the real world. By real world we mean the messy, complex, changing, and unpredictable organizations such as the one you probably are part of.

In summary, our approaches are based on experience, review of academic literature and practical application. Before we move on to how Quality organizations can be structured to better reflect or support some of the approaches described in this book, it is worth reflecting on how Quality organizations currently look. Understanding how we got here helps immensely in understanding where you need to go, and the challenges you will face.

Quality: How Is It Structured?

It would be true to say that while quality management as an approach isn't the Wild West, there are currently few rules on how you approach it or how you structure your organization. In certain industries, the Quality function must be independent of manufacturing and an individual appointed to oversee the organization. Aside from that there is no regulatory mandate that dictates how a Quality organization is organized, either in its size structure or the skill sets it has within it. In many ways, regulators leave it to businesses to how they organize themselves to best meet the regulations.

If you look at a range of companies, you will, however, see common themes around how Quality organizations are set up. You will see Supplier Quality, which deals with incoming inspection and suppliers; Quality Assurance, which focuses on how the products are designed and manufactured consistently to meet customer expectations, as well as other functions that are focused on regulatory compliance in addition to other groups dedicated to other parts of the QMS.

As an example, one function that is seen in a range of organizations is the Quality Engineering organization. The role and purpose of this group will be highly dependent on which organization you look at. In certain organizations they are akin to custodians of the QMS. In others, this function focuses on controlling nonconforming product and in other organizations they have a more continuous improvement role. This same group across different businesses may look very different.

Similarly, if you peered into any one Quality organization and looked at the qualifications and experience of those who work there you would see a very broad spectrum of individuals. Many will have a technical background. Others will have come from manufacturing, while some may have come from a regulatory or compliance background. While degrees and diplomas in Quality are available and are becoming more popular, certainly within the healthcare industry, it is somewhat uncommon for leaders within the Quality organization to have formal qualifications in the discipline.

This aspect of differing roles, range of qualifications gives those that work in the Quality arena a somewhat weaker sense of self-identity, compared with other professions. This has been long noted for a while by those that look at organizations [40]. Entry into Quality is generally not via professional certification, such as seen in other occupations such as finance and law. This has resulted in a variability of approach in a field that itself can be interpreted multiple ways.

This is not to say that the status is right or wrong. It just reflects where Quality organizations are. The positive news, however, is that it does offer huge potential in how Quality organizations could be organized. Essentially, it gives you very broad scope for change.

Before we go on to talk about Quality organizations specifically, it helps if we cover some of the recent opinions, discussion, and evidence of how organizations in general are undergoing change. This is particularly relevant, as no industry is totally immune from the impact of technological advances, and sociological and demographic changes. However, it can be difficult to separate out what is evidence-based opinion from that which is speculation, hype, or even just flagrant misinformation.

So, the World of Work Is Changing—or Is It?

One of the consistent messages in business today is that virtually all modern organizations operate in what is known as a knowledge-based economy. Organizations compete for individuals with the best intelligence and qualifications, and through these "knowledge workers" the business gains competitive advantage.

Some have argued that the concept of a "knowledge economy" and "knowledge workers" is largely a mirage [41]. While such aspirations are laudable—using the intellectual power of your staff—most workers generally do not have the opportunity to apply their intelligence or creativity on a day-to-day basis. Often, they are asked to perform tasks well below their intellectual ability and qualifications. In the healthcare industry, those working in a hospital laboratory or a manufacturing facility 30 years ago would have been school leavers with good exam results. Today they often need a degree or postgraduate qualification to be considered for employment.

In 2008, two sociologists, Sweet and Meiksins, performed an extensive study of U.S. workplaces looking at research reports from many hundreds of work environments. A shiny new economy, replete with knowledge workers was simply nowhere to be found [42]. Low-level service jobs still dominated. Highly paid, highly skilled knowledge workers were rare. Even organizations that we would consider to be on the cutting edge of technology such as IBM, most of their staff worked in call centers and offices executing rather mundane activities. This finding of general job deskilling was confirmed with a further study in 2020 [43].

As a leader responsible for a Quality organization does this matter?

Yes.

As a leader you should question whether all the positions within your jurisdiction are making valid contributions to delivering customer value. Are they doing tasks that add value for the customers of the QMS? Are they using the skills appropriately? Are they being suitably developed?

While there are several tasks within the QMS that can be automated, there are still many tasks that need people, especially those involving making a risk-based judgment using incomplete data.

In recent years there has been great emphasis on the application of technology within the QMS, and there is probably not a day that goes by where you are not bombarded with e-mails selling the latest technological advancement. There has been lesser focus on the people skills and competencies your organization needs. Importantly, these are attributes that will set you apart from other organizations.

You need to ensure that all positions in the Quality organization reflect the job being done, one that is needed, and importantly, one that fully employs the intellectual capacity of your staff. Technology is a means to them achieving this task rather than the goal. But let's explore this aspect of technology a little further. Within quality management it has caused an industry of, some would say "smoke and mirrors," to be spawned in its own right.

Industry 4.0 > Quality 4.0?

If you do a Google search for "Industry 4.0" you get 2.8 billion hits. Suffice to say the question of whether we are in the midst of a fourth industrial revolution or not is largely irrelevant. The Internet has spoken.

It is worth covering some of the aspects of Industry 4.0, as it extends to the potential impact of what has been called Quality 4.0. It is also important as it sets the context of different capabilities and competences your organization will need going forward.

The phrase "Industry 4.0" was originally proposed by the German government and covers an age triggered by technological innovation [44]. Industry 4.0 is underpinned by the arrival of e-connected manufacturing systems, the availability of big data, artificial intelligence (AI), and machine learning.

The 1st Industrial Revolution covered the invention of the steam engine. The 2nd Industrial Revolution, electrification of factories, while the 3rd Industrial Revolution was the result of the invention of the microprocessor. There are those that argue the advent of increased data and ability to mine the data—often in real time—constitutes an age that warrants classification as a 4th industrial period.

There are also counterarguments that claim we are not experiencing a new age warranting special classification, despite the plethora of publications and publicity around the concept.

Stretching the analogy of Industry 4.0 further, several commentators have termed the concept Quality 4.0, which is essentially the application of digital technology in the context of the QMS [45, 46].

The increased availability of quality data with the potential to make more predictive assessments of product performance does support the idea that the role of the Quality professional will change [47]. There are certainly examples that can be used to validate the idea of Quality 4.0 as a concept. These include better understanding of in-process data, remote monitoring of products in the customer's hands, and even the ability to predict product performance that would precede a customer complaint.

While the impact of information technology and AI has huge potential to impact the quality system, the primary questions you as a leader probably have when faced with the deluge of information heralding this brand-new age are the following.

Will the application of approaches defined in Quality 4.0 really benefit the customers of the QMS? Will the benefits from applying these approaches be outweighed by the resources I have available?

Essentially, does implementing the approaches covered under Quality 4.0 give me the competitive advantage, cost reduction, quality improvement, or increased regulated compliance to justify the body of work to deliver them? There are also secondary questions about whether you have the required skill sets in your organization, and whether these approaches need to be planned and implemented now, or form part of a medium/longer term approach.

Certainly, organizations that have significant resource, able to deliver economies of scale and at the technological cutting edge will be better placed to exploit the concepts of Quality 4.0. However, most companies are small. They have neither bandwidth nor the capabilities to incorporate such analysis into their day-to-day operations. In Europe, the medical technology sector comprises over 33,000 companies. While technologically advanced, greater than 95 percent of these businesses are small to medium enterprises with less than 250 staff [48].

In summary, the QMS will certainly develop as technology changes, but probably won't result in a step change for most organizations in the short term. Be aware of the changes in your industry and the aspects you need to incorporate now, but don't be driven by the technology.

So, what about leadership? What changes may be needed to align with some of the content we have covered? What is the best leadership approach?

Leadership

This is an aspect we touched on in the previous chapter. There are a wide range of leadership approaches. The business sections of bookstores are heavy with texts detailing different, and often contradictory approaches of how best to lead organizations. These include authentic, value-based, servant-based, transformational, charismatic, facilitative, situational, and so on. The list goes on.

The purpose of this book is not to dictate which leadership style or approach is most valid. Though we would state that servant-based leadership has strong merits [39], your own leadership style will depend on a combination of your experience, personal preference, psychological makeup, and latest trend in the leadership industry. In addition, one of the general themes of leadership is that it is also contextual. Certain organizations at different periods of their development benefit from different leadership approaches. In addition, even within a given organization the approach to leading may be highly dependent on those you will be asking to be followers.

There are several leadership themes that during a transformation of a quality organization will make your job easier and be more consistent with the messages in this book. Approaches that encourage collaboration, critical thinking, and reflection are well suited to the material covered. It is relevant, however, to quickly reflect how your direct reports—who in general will be managers and directors—behave in organizations.

In 1988 Robert Jackal in his book, *Moral Mazes*, performed an extensive study of life within large U.S. corporations [49]. He interviewed middle managers to understand how they behaved in the corporate environment. Several themes stood out. Generally, success within an organization was dictated by managers following a rather limited set of simple rules:

1. Never go around your boss.
2. Even when your boss claims they want diverse and at times dissenting views, essentially always tell your boss what they want to hear.
3. If your boss wants something to stop happening, it stops happening.

4. Anticipate your boss's needs, such that they do not have to behave as a boss.
5. Do what the job needs and at times simply keep your mouth shut.

As you can see, successful managers in large organizations do not generally succeed and move up the career ladder by asking questions, critically thinking, or going through periods of self-reflection. This somewhat puts the messages in this book at odds with the required behaviors for successful career progression of not only your direct reports but also yourself.

The way to help break this paradox is to both understand that it exists and also recognize it around you. Also, take a step back and remember your principal role as a Quality leader is to protect your customers, your business, and your organization's regulatory reputation. Generally, successful career progression is simply a by-product of getting these correct both for you and your reports.

People, Process, and Technology

Splitting the system out into People, Process, and Technology is a convenient and often-used way of looking at organizations. It can also be applied to the QMS as a means of looking at it through different eyes. At times, there is overlap between the three areas, as individuals follow processes through application of technology to execute the quality system (Figure 7.1).

People

One of the analogies used in business to build an effective organization is that you need to get the right people on the bus, the wrong people off the bus, and everybody sitting in the right seats to have any chance of reaching your destination [50].

This section covers the capabilities that you will need, how to organize them, and how to influence that often nebulous concept of culture.

Undoubtedly, the best way of having an efficient and effective quality system is to automate it. However, not all the QMS can be automated nor should it be. Even with advances in AI there are aspects that need

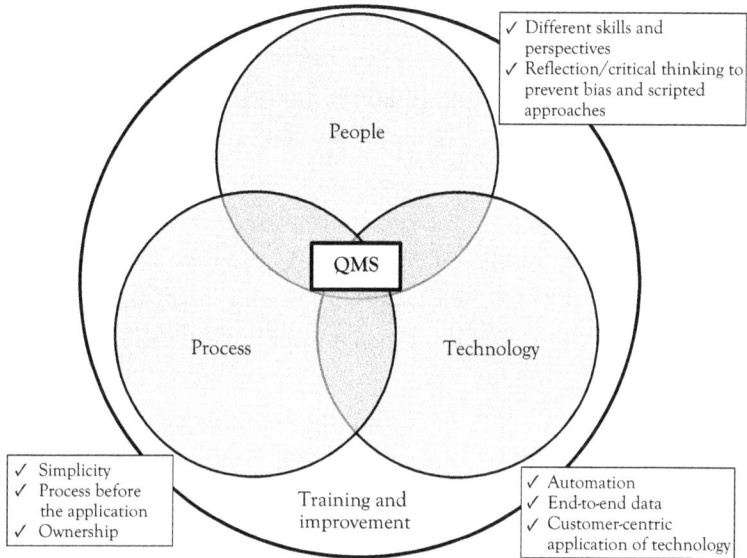

Figure 7.1 The three dimensions of the QMS

people and their ability to make decisions based on experience, wisdom, and context. So, you need people, and you'll need them for two reasons.

First, getting things done, and secondly getting things done in the way that you want them to get done. This brings us to two aspects: competencies and behaviors. Combined they contribute somewhat to the often hazy notion: culture.

It is critical you are selfish in the outcomes you expect from the QMS. You expect it to create safe, high-quality products that are financially successful and in doing so you obey the law. You're going to have to deliver these outcomes through people.

You need to take an interest in people. Less so because you want to be seen as a nice guy and people person. It is because through people your quality system lives and breathes.

Skills and Competencies

If you look around your current organization, you will generally see common themes in terms of competencies. There are fields of expertise that require formal qualification. These include statistics, data analysis, information technology, and so on.

It does help if you encourage a degree of diversity in your organization. Bringing different perspectives together is not to create some utopian politically correct, diverse population, but bringing together dissimilar, and often challenging, opinions will help you make better decisions, with access to the skills you need.

Moreover, skills that were needed yesterday may not be those required for the Quality organization of the future. A process thinking approach, comfortable and able to understand limited data, needs to be replaced with a systems / complexity thinking approach with the skills to humanize big data.

In addition to skill sets, it is also important how people apply their knowledge and how they interact collectively. The Quality organization is more than a collection of discrete individuals. How they achieve tasks is as important as what they achieve. Their behaviors can make or break your organization.

Behaviors

The human brain has a lot to deal with on a day-to-day basis. To prevent cognitive overload, evolution has developed a series of tricks and tools to lighten the load. We all hold cognitive biases and often cherry-pick information to validate a preconceived notion. We base events and how we respond to them on what has worked well in the past.

In addition, we operate scripts that we execute to make life easier. These are essentially rules of thumb of how we should behave and deal in any given situation. We employ them when we interact with each other, with our family and friends and, to a large extent, ourselves.

It is impossible for you to employ anybody who does not have some form of cognitive bias or follows such scripts. Essentially, they would not be human. It is, however, possible to encourage behaviors you want to see and make all individuals aware of the potential for their own bias blind spots, and tendency to react to scenarios in a scripted and standard manner. The mitigation is to embrace more reflective approaches and critical thinking.

The more you can do this, the more you can protect yourself from risk: risk to your customers, your business, your organization's regulatory position, and your own personal reputation.

In addition, Quality organizations require different behaviors to those that have previously been successful. Whilst before a quality professional needed to be factory facing, putting compliance first, policing stakeholders; now they need to be customer facing, putting customers' needs first with the ability to mentor, coach and partner with stakeholders.

Process and Procedures

People like processes. For many industries, the process needs to be something more than in your head. It needs to be written down. Most importantly, it needs to be clear enough that it can be consistently executed by others. The enemy of quality is variation, and the cause of variation is often unclear expectations and instructions to meet them.

Writing procedures that describe processes in a manner such that they are consistently executed is notoriously difficult. There are several rules to follow that help. The first is simplicity. If you can build your process as simple as possible, it will not only be easier to describe but also easier to execute. Often there is tendency to create documents with pages and pages of fine detail, in the belief that this will make the process more secure. It will not. In practice, it will create a myriad of ways the document can be misinterpreted. In addition, you will create a compliance timebomb as you struggle to demonstrate, with objective evidence, you were following your own procedures. When creating procedures, the questions you need to have in your mind are: Do I really need this instruction and is it clear?

Gone are the days where instructions and procedures relied only on words. Now you can easily supplement them with graphics, photos, and videos to demonstrate how the procedure should be executed. Ideally, these work instructions should be visible/accessible within the workplace. A clear well-defined procedure is useless if it is buried away in a filing cabinet or deep within the folders of your document management system.

Even if the procedure is clear and the process waste free, who does it belong to?

The issue is around accountability and ownership. Many organizations have procedures, or even whole processes that are critical to the execution of the quality system with no defined owners. This results in procedures that are prone to diverging from reality of execution, becoming out of date, and not being maintained.

You need to define specific individuals with accountability and responsibility for maintaining specific documents and procedures. Most importantly, these individuals need to have explicit knowledge of the execution of the process. You need at least one person who understands the process or procedure and will be the expert to explain it during an inspection.

The next issue around processes is related to their connectivity. As detailed in the previous chapter, processes interact to form a system. You need to ensure that the connections between subsystems of the QMS are clear and describable, ideally presented graphically.

The final aspect and one that's reared its head over the last 10 to 15 years is the role of electronic quality management systems (e-QMSs). Electronic systems are the future and any organization still using a wholly paper-based quality system needs to join the 21st century. There are, however, several watchouts.

First, ensure that you have a clear process defined on paper before you move it to an electronic system. Beware of quality system projects turning into IT delivery exercises. It is easy to hardwire a bad process into your e-QMS in the excitement of going through a technological step change. Secondly, it may feel more satisfying to have your subsystems within a single application (e.g.: an enterprise resource planning (ERP) tool), but will it compromise usability in doing so? Generally, this is to help data move through the system with ease. If it doesn't help, then standardization for standardization's sake has no benefit for the customer. Many ERP applications can be used to incorporate QMS modules such as CAPA, audit, and nonconformance, but in doing so they can lose a large degree of end-user usability especially where specific configuration is costly. Do not underestimate the importance of a user-friendly interface that encourages use of the application rather than making it a stressful and frustrating effort.

Finally, whatever vendors may say, do not confuse the electronic application with your quality system. These are transactional tools to help you execute your QMS and no more.

Training and Improvement

Having simple processes that are clearly described is not enough. This is especially true for steps that are critical within the manufacturing process which impact the quality and safety of your products. You will need to train individuals in how to execute processes and as importantly they need to demonstrate understanding and the ability to carry out tasks appropriately.

The importance of effective training can be traced back to initiatives such as Training Within Industry (TWI) developed during the Second World War and as such these approaches are experiencing a degree of resurgence.

The TWI approach to training is characterized by four attributes:

1. Simplicity. There is particular focus on getting the job done.
2. Focus. The training should involve the minimum of training time.
3. Learning by doing. Training focuses on hands on demonstration of the training being applied.
4. Cascaded. There is an expectation that those trained provide training to others in a cascade effect.

While such an approach was designed to meet the urgency and need of WWII, the system of training still has substantial merits and is training in its purest form, devoid of any extraneous material. Despite its age, it is still a model worth considering for all organizations.

Like many approaches we have covered so far, the importance with training is that it should be proportionate. Not every change to every document requires extensive training and assessment.

When developing training programs there is generally a focus on the QMS. However, there are many skills that while not directly associated with the QMS, have a huge impact on the quality of your organization. These include the ability to write clear and concise reports, the ability to manage projects effectively, and the ability to facilitate meetings and present data efficiently. In addition, there are competencies such as soft skills, like the ability to influence and cognitive skills such as critical thinking and reflexivity. Do not underestimate the value of incorporating these areas into your quality training program.

One of the aspects of measuring quality system effectiveness is the general focus on quantitative measures. These areas are easier to quantify. Though at times they may not be measures of system output, more a measure of system activity, a review of a QSMR deck will generally have quantitative measures for each of the components of the quality system.

There is, however, an equivalent qualitative mirror that often goes unreviewed. For example, when measuring the CAPA process we often focus on the number of events, the number that are overdue, and their cycle time. We rarely look at more qualitative aspects of the CAPA process, such as the ease of access of the data, the clarity of the reporting, the ease of use of the application by the end user. Rarely do we incorporate such measures of process effectiveness into the quality system review, as they are more challenging to quantify, but no less important. Any CAPA system is useless if nobody wants to use it.

Conversely, throughout the execution of the quality system we often give and receive qualitative feedback, such as the quality of reports, meetings, data presentation, and so on. Often this feedback is vague. For example, "this report needs a bit of work" can be interpreted as either it only requires minor edits, or it needs extensive revision. Think about being more quantitative in your feedback.

For example, telling an individual that the quality of their technical report scored as 2 out of 10 for clarity, should drive a conversation about aspects that are absent or could be strengthened. Conversely, a score of 9 would support that the report is suitable. Consider incorporating some degree of quantitation to at least drive conversations that are less nebulous and less likely to be misinterpreted. This aspect is important because without it there can be no conversation around gaps in quality, and subsequently no learning or improvement. Again, the purpose is not to demoralize or criticize individuals. It is to make sure that your quality system better delivers for all its customers.

Technology

Technological approaches should be used within the QMS if it helps the delivery of customer value, be it increasing efficiency, error proofing to enhance compliance and safety, or better understanding the operation of the QMS. Technology should not be applied just for technology's sake. Technology can be used to improve the QMS user experience, automate repetitive tasks, or help to visualize the data within your business.

Again, the customers of QMS are your reference points. You should refer to them when considering application of technology. Will it help them or not?

The other watchout is that technology may solve one problem but create another. For example, electronic batch records are notoriously difficult to maintain with respect to change control. The gains achieved by applying electronic systems often come at an unexpected business cost.

The Quality Organization of the Future

It would be remiss of this chapter not to discuss the future of Quality. Much focus has been around the impact of Quality 4.0 and the aspects of technology such as AI, robotics, and big data. Without doubt, these advances will have an impact on all manufacturing organizations and service providers.

In truth, the role of Quality organization has always evolved. Initially the focus was on inspection and defect removal. This then moved to focusing more on designing quality into the product, as opposed to weeding defects out. Areas such as Six Sigma saw focus on cause-and-effect approaches, design of experiments to test hypotheses, and identify corrective actions. This then led to where Quality functions are now.

Going forward, there will be more exploratory approaches based on data analysis, often operating in real time, and these technology advances will certainly impact how quality is managed by Quality organizations. You will still need people who can apply their intelligence and inquisitively explore how the data can be turned into wisdom.

That is not to say, each phase replaces the previous approach but builds on and supplements what were once former state-of-the-art ways to improving quality (see Figure 7.2).

In essence, the purpose of the Quality professional will also change, given both the increase in regulations, expectations of continuous improvement and the increased application of technology. The Quality professional has moved away from a policing role to being custodians of the QMS under frameworks such as TQM. In recent years there has been particular focus on quality improvement methodologies, such as lean and Six Sigma, with Quality taking a very engineering focused view of the

Quality as Inspection	Quality as Design	Quality as Experimentation	Quality as Discovery
Quality driven by inspection and defect removal.	Quality driven by design quality into the product.	Quality driven by root cause analysis, hypothesis testing, and corrective and preventive action.	Quality driven by exploration of data sets, application of artificial intelligence to gain new insights.

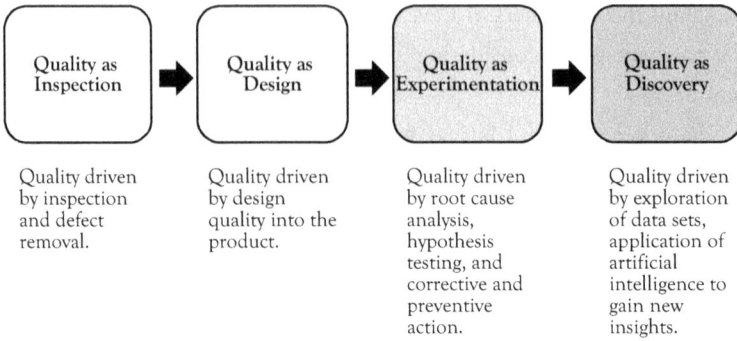

Figure 7.2 Evolution of approaches to Quality

Source: Reproduced by permission of *The American Society for Quality* [51].

world. Going forward, Quality will certainly take a more enabling role, using a variety of approaches to better understand the ways and means of improving quality (see Figure 7.3).

To gain a more objective assessment of where Quality is going, in 2019 researchers and practitioners held an extensive workshop, under the direction of the Swedish Institute for Quality. This comprised both a brainstorming workshop and an appreciative inquiry summit to determine the future research themes for quality management, looking toward a date line of 2030.

The participants were all active members of the Quality community, directly involved in driving quality management search and education.

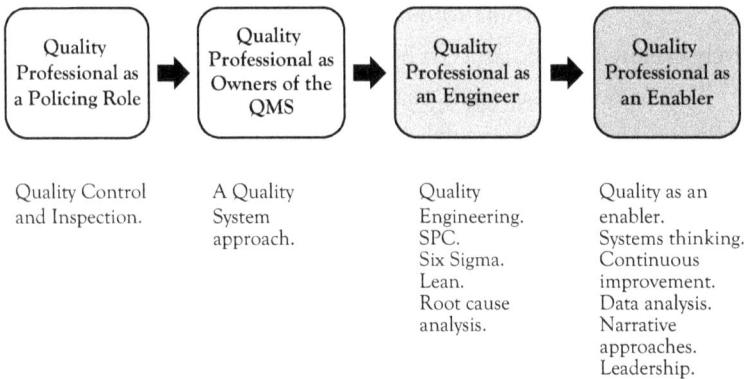

Quality Professional as a Policing Role	Quality Professional as Owners of the QMS	Quality Professional as an Engineer	Quality Professional as an Enabler
Quality Control and Inspection.	A Quality System approach.	Quality Engineering. SPC. Six Sigma. Lean. Root cause analysis.	Quality as an enabler. Systems thinking. Continuous improvement. Data analysis. Narrative approaches. Leadership.

Figure 7.3 The evolving role of the Quality professional

They offer a somewhat independent view of the trajectory of travel of the role of Quality going forward and do offer some insight into the research agenda to come [52].

The workshop and summit identified five themes for quality management, going forward. These can be broadly summarized as: (1) A systems approach; (2) control versus change; (3) sustainability; (4) the greater why, and (5) organizational flexibility.

If we review these five areas it will give some clarity of how they through the three organizational categories—People, Process, and Technology—may impact Quality organizations, going forward. In the next section we will consider each of these in more detail, with practical aspects of how this may translate into changes that can be considered for your Quality organization, as shown in Table 7.1.

A Systems Approach

There are two practical consequences of looking at the QMS as a holistic and complex system. First is the obvious need to articulate this view to those that plan, implement, and maintain aspects of the quality system. This may require a degree of revision of a machine-dominated vision of the world. Second is the acceptance that a system is continually changing and adapting. This has several direct consequences. Approaches to understanding the system through experimentation are less successful or at times impossible. Appreciation of the system is needed before decisions are made, to determine whether the state under review is simple, complicated, complex, or even chaotic.

A systems view of the QMS also drives a different perspective regarding assessing effectiveness, adequacy, and suitability of the quality system. In many respects, QSMR is a snapshot-in-time based on historic data. To be fully effective, QSMR needs to be more forward looking, understanding both the lagging and leading indicators of quality and use a customer's perspective of value, to truly understand the system effectiveness. Seeing the QMS as a system also puts particular emphasis on how technology is applied. Having isolated data silos makes it challenging to see the links between inputs and outputs.

Table 7.1 The future of quality management

	People	Process	Technology
A Systems approach	☐ Train in systems thinking and the ability to make decisions based on situational context. ☐ Supplement engineering approaches with other world-views.	☐ Broaden the scope of end-to-end quality and associated data. ☐ See the quality system, organization, and environment as being interconnected. ☐ See Quality System Management Review as value adding and only a snapshot in time. Be forward- as well as backward-looking.	☐ Move toward a single eco-system for data and processes. ☐ Have systems that can handle and able to mine both quantitative and qualitative data.
Control versus Change	☐ Hire both "controllers" and "innovators." ☐ Create diverse teams but allow individuals to play to their strengths. ☐ Reward the ability to work in situations of uncertainty. ☐ Train in practical approaches required to take a risk-based approach: behaviors and technical tools. ☐ Train in the ability to assess the benefit and cost of change. ☐ Leaders act through example.	☐ Do not implement one-size fits all for standardization's sake. ☐ Implement scalable processes that are flexible and contingent on the situation and issue. ☐ Have processes that are not only proactive and able to influence the system but also have the ability to react to signals. ☐ Incorporate aspects of ISO56000 series around innovation management into quality management.	☐ Improve access to all the data needed to support risk-based decision making.

Sustainability	☐ Develop "Life Cycle Engineers." ☐ Deploy training and awareness of the sustainability dimensions: economic, social, ecological and the impact of the quality system on these.	☐ Include aspects of sustainability as part of Quality System Management Review: Cost, human resources, impact of manufacturing and distribution footprint, recyclability, and compliance with ISO14000 standards.	☐ Improve access to actionable intelligence covering end-to-end supply chain.
The greater **Why**	☐ Communicate the importance of all of the quality system's three customers: customer experience, business sustainability, and compliance. ☐ Communicate the ability of the quality system to create a greater good.	☐ Understand customer needs and truly connect with them. ☐ Understand what it means to be a satisfied customer. ☐ Implement outcome-driven metrics.	☐ Create the ability to differentiate between data, information, knowledge, and wisdom. ☐ Go beyond the use of quantitative data to gain true insight.
Organizational **Flexibility**	☐ Train the organization in the concepts and practice of empowerment. ☐ Set challenges rather than deploying solutions. ☐ Develop people skills. ☐ Encourage free flow of communication. ☐ Break down functional silos.	☐ Drive collaboration with practical changes: multifunctional work centers, Quality on the production floor, multifunctional forums at all levels of the organization. ☐ Drive decision making down to the appropriate level.	☐ Deploy tools to increase collaborative and communication.

Data needs to be translated into wisdom. This requires a more holistic view of data analysis, using not only both traditional quantitative approaches but also more narrative methods such as interviewing and feedback.

The quality system is not a machine but has powerful political, social, and cultural aspects that have huge impact on its ability to satisfy customer need.

Questions to be asked are as follows:

- What is the current state of the system under review?
- How will interventions impact other aspects of the system?
- How is the complete system and its constituent parts adding value and satisfying customer need?
- How is waste manifesting itself in the system?

Control Versus Change

The dilemma at the heart of all quality system frameworks is the requirement to balance stability and regulatory control with the need for change and innovation. This requires not only your quality system but also you as a leader, to be ambidextrous in delivering opposing outcomes.

To achieve this, you will need to hire a range of skill sets, big picture thinkers, and those with an eye for detail. Neither type of approach is better than the other. This will mean opening the QMS up to more innovative ways of doing things, while using risk management approaches to assess and mitigate risk. Again, do not drive change for change's sake but to better deliver often shifting and increasing customer expectations.

This will require you to lead by example. You will have to demonstrate that you can make pragmatic risk-based decisions and as importantly be able to articulate your rationale behind them to your organization. You will have to demonstrate an ability to change course and adjust your plans as circumstances dictate. Key will be the ability to think critically and overcome inherent biases in the decision-making process. At times you will make wrong decisions. You will need to use these as exercises in self-reflection and learning, and demonstrate to your organization the value of doing so.

Sustainability

Your jurisdiction as a leader no longer starts and ends at the factory gate. The impact of the products you design, manufacture, and distribute extends from your suppliers, right through to how your products are disposed of by the end user. You will need to change your approach with individuals who can see the whole flow.

Develop life cycle engineers responsible for both the life cycle of the product, from design, manufacturing, to obsolescence, as well as the life cycle of individual lots from the raw materials used, to disposal or recycling of the final product. Quality as a function needs to think holistically and be better integrated into all aspects of the business and this includes environmental sustainability.

QSMR is a must do for all Quality organizations and is effective in (1) monitoring lagging and leading signals, (2) assessing risk, and (3) applying appropriate mitigations. It is equally suited to monitoring the effectiveness of environmental management and sustainability. These aspects should be incorporated into a more balanced QSMR process, covering aspects that are generally not considered, such as suppliers' sustainability credentials, human resource and environmental impact of manufacturing, distribution, and end-user use of products. It could be argued that environmental standards such as ISO14001 could be covered as part of a more holistic review of organizational quality [53].

The Greater Why

This next area talks to why any of us come to work, volunteer, or involve ourselves in any activity with others. Some are in employment simply to earn money. It is a transaction between the employer and the employee, no more and no less. For these individuals there is no interest in the greater good or the organization. It matters little whether the business makes paper clips, pharmaceuticals, or military hardware.

For a Quality organization to have a higher purpose, the first port of call is to explain that quality does not equate to just compliance. The function is responsible for more than adherence to regulations. If you have an organization that believes this is their prime purpose you will have to address this head on, messy as this may be. Some individuals may need to get off the bus.

Articulating the three main customers of the quality system and regularly repeating this message is one clear, practical, and positive step forward to moving the QMS to having a broader purpose. A consequence of multiple customers of the QMS is also truly understanding their needs.

The questions you should be asking yourself as a leader and your organization, are: What does it truly mean to be a satisfied customer? How will I measure this? How can I impact it positively?

To answer these questions, you are going to have to go beyond simple numeric data and translating data in all its forms—quantitative and narrative—to gain insight on how best to focus the quality system under your direction to meet its customers' needs.

Organizational Flexibility

None of us knows what the future holds. Certainly, the experience of the past few years has demonstrated this profoundly. Few would argue against the view that the future does look increasingly challenging for all organizations. With respect to how you organize a Quality function is directly linked to how you allow your organization to make decisions.

As covered previously, there are a wide range of leadership styles, each with its own specific pros and cons. While there are scenarios where a "command-and-control" approach maybe the best solution such as the armed forces or firefighting, generally such an approach will be highly rigid and too slow to react to hidden signals. At the other extreme, an organization where there are no rules or management layers, while applicable to certain industries such as the creative arts, do not work in organizations where products or services must be delivered in a consistent and reliable manner.

Again, the organization must have sufficient structure to be consistent, but not being so rigid such that it cannot react to changing events. Research does show that the appropriate leadership style for many organizations is one that enables and supports some degree of self-organization [54].

But what does this mean in practice?

First, you need to encourage the free flow of communication and consequently access to the data as covered previously. You also need to attempt to break down functional silos. For example, you need to embed your Quality organization in situ within the manufacturing process, rather than having it isolated as a back-office function. Quality staff need to be located in the processes they support; if not, then Quality becomes little more than a nonvalue adding remote operation.

In addition, you will need to ensure that your organization can make decisions at the appropriate level. There will need to be a clear understanding of what needs to be escalated up through the management chain versus what can be resolved locally. This also accepts that there will be instances where individuals will make incorrect calls, and issues may appear hidden from you as a leader. This is a lesser risk than you becoming swamped with a thousand minor issues each day as your organization becomes unable to make pragmatic, risk-based decisions at the level of the organization they are needed. Significant improvements can be made by learning from organizations that deal with more pressing and critical challenges.

Several organizations have implemented approaches that mimic the ways in which agencies react to disasters. For example, the use of predefined protocols detailing the agreed action plan and requiring all stakeholders with decision-making authority to meet rapidly in the place where the issue under investigation has occurred. These predefined reaction plans, with a clear mechanism by which to document information, visible to all parties, ensures that critical events are addressed swiftly in a collaborative and nonsequential manner. Quality organizations have a real role to play in not only being part of such approaches but also leading when the issue at hand is related to product quality.

In summary, as we reviewed the five ways that Quality organizations are thought to change over the coming years, you will notice there is little mention of e-QMSs, AI, robotics, or big data. While these will undoubtedly play a role in quality organizations going forward, they are a means to an end, as opposed to the end themselves. The purpose of the quality system is to ensure that the organization obeys applicable laws, meets customers' needs and expectations, and adds value to the business.

Summary

To build a successful Quality organization you need to address the processes, the people who must follow them, and the technology that enables them to do so.

- Seek diversity and allow individuals to play to their strengths.
- Do not chase technology for technology's sake.
- Beware of the myth of standardization.
- Center the organization and QMS around delivering customers' needs.
- Develop wisdom through critical thinking and reflection.

CHAPTER 8

Implementing a Quality Organization Transformation

Everyone wants to do a good job according to their understanding of what "quality" means to them. The problem is that "quality" is often a subjective interpretation. This is an important concept to begin this chapter with, because essentially it is all about winning hearts and minds in making a change for the better. If you start from a position of "they don't know what they are doing," you will fail. In many respects, planning, executing, and maintaining a quality transformation is an exercise in answering the following:

- Why?
- What and When?
- And How?

The Why?—a Culture of Quality

It begins as a collective exercise in understanding. You should start with questioning yourself as a quality leader as to why you are commencing such a difficult task in the first place. Many leaders probably don't even attempt to put together a plan, as there is no short-term political gain, which comes back to the need for prerequisite support from above and the ability for leadership—and you—to see a better future. There are companies where the culture is intrinsically linked to the products they make. Individuals see the direct impact on peoples' lives. This is not true for all businesses, even in healthcare.

If individuals see no connection between their daily activity and an outcome for the customer, then the task of creating a transformational map becomes more difficult, as you then need to address your "Culture of Quality" [55, 56].

In writing a book on transforming Quality organizations it is not possible to ignore the topic of "Culture of Quality." Merriam Webster defines culture as "the set of shared attitudes, values, goals, and practices that characterizes an institution or organization." In life, these are engrained into us from an early age and define the behavioral norms we see and feel every day. How do you replicate this within a quality system?

In the process of defining why you need to commence a Quality transformation, there needs to be a crystal clear understanding of what your products are, and the expectations your customers have of them. Most importantly, every individual at every level needs to understand their contribution in the task of meeting this expectation. You also need to articulate the different customers of the quality system that we have covered within this book.

In truth, many business leaders rarely touch or are directly involved in their products either during the design, creation, or distribution phases. It is at the coalface lower down the organization that real "value" is created. One critical mistake a business leader can make is to both over and underestimate their ability to influence this value creation.

To this end, it is of little value if you, as a leader, understand the concepts described in this book, if you do not instill the expectation within your organization, at all levels, that compliance, end customer experience, and cost are all customers that are served by the QMS, and through their day to day actions, they can influence this.

Not all products save lives, some products give customer satisfaction, others just meet a need. Whatever the product or service you deliver the first step in creating a culture of quality is to articulate to your organization the value of your offering. You need to do this through more than slogans or generic messaging. Importantly, you will need, at some point, to involve somebody else: the customer.

Practical ways of doing this include connecting your end customers directly with your organization, building a closer relationship between your supply chain partners and your business, and opening a window to your organization as to how your products are used in the real world.

We have witnessed many times the impact and power of real customers presenting to the entire company on the consequence of products not working as expected, and the direct impact it can have on the life of a patient. We have also witnessed the power that comes when a customer explains how a product is used to make a positive, life changing difference. Connecting to the customer is a remarkable driver in the pursuit of quality.

Through your daily words and actions as a leader, you set an example of the behaviors you'll support, and those that you will not tolerate. Through your behaviors you build the cultural environment within your organization, for better or worse. As a leader you need to be clear, consistent, and continuous in your messaging about the importance and criticality of quality to your business.

In the process of explaining the "why," some individuals will certainly get it, others will not, and others will just pretend to be on board. It is important to state that laying the foundations for a culture of quality is not a process of brainwashing or attempting to force individuals to think in a particular way, which often can only give the illusion of mass acceptance. It is more a process of giving individuals the appropriate information such that they can make informed choices of how they best contribute or not. Often "hats and badges" initiatives simply fail because they attempt to force a culture and way of thinking onto an organization in a way that is shallow and unsustainable.

So, if you attempt to execute a quality transformation without doing some groundwork in establishing a culture of quality, or don't already have an organization that is receptive, then you are likely to fail. There are three basic elements that we feel are critical:

- Executive champions
- Empowered and engaged employees
- A learning culture

Executive Champions

It starts at the top. It is critical that you secure executive buy in. Many Six Sigma initiatives fail as the project sponsor, while proclaiming to support the project is a distant and disinterested individual. You are going to have to get them engaged. In many respects, the position you take with your sponsor will be dependent on their perspective. The goal might be to effect a cultural change, or it might be driven by pure business metrics. In short, you need to know what your audience want.

Leadership being seen to embrace quality needs to be visible and felt by the entire workforce. It should be aligned and core to the purpose of the organization. It needs to feature prominently in the goals/objectives of the organization and be evident in its strategy. Practical examples demonstrating this include the following:

- The quality policy should be on display. It should be simple enough for employees to remember the key messages. It should also make it clear that its obligations apply equally to all employees.
- In executive meetings, quality should be one of the first topics on the agenda and not relegated to the end. If employees see that quality is discussed front and center at the executive level, they are more likely to position it similarly themselves.
- In company town halls, the topic of quality should be one of the first discussed and the CEO must be seen taking the lead in discussing its importance to the business.
- Finally, as a watchpoint, an idle comment can do untold harm and undermine all your efforts. In 1991, Gerald Ratner, the CEO of a UK high-street jeweler, made a publicly disparaging comment on the quality of his companies' products. He single-handedly destroyed trust and faith and led the closure of a major high-street brand.

Key learnings from our experience include:

- Make sure you know your executive audience and approach the topic of transformation accordingly.
- Don't over commit at this stage.
- This is a marathon, not a sprint, so take your time.
- Often, the executive audience doesn't even know there is a problem.

Empowered and Engaged Employees

Many organizations talk about employee empowerment with decisions being made at the appropriate level. As previously covered, this does require leadership to relinquish a degree of control. Which may, at times, be uncomfortable for you. At times you will get views that are difficult to hear.

If leadership is genuinely bought into the concept of a culture of quality, then employees need to be able to voice concerns about its aspects. No ifs. No buts.

There also needs to be evidence that concerns are being actively heard and responded to. Many organizations proclaim a "no-blame" culture. This is far easier to say than make happen, but larger organizations than yours have made it happen. The requirement for full transparency and a culture where admitting mistakes is actively encouraged, is nowhere more important than within healthcare if true improvements in patient safety are to be made [57].

Practical ways to demonstrate commitment to an open culture include continuous improvement/suggestion schemes that are clearly visible in the workplace and regularly reviewed by leadership.

Employees are the few who really create value in businesses, and they should own their procedures and processes. The act of forgetting that staff are the subject matter experts can itself be a lost opportunity. There are many organizations where the bulk of procedures are owned by the Quality unit, simply because the procedures are part of the quality system. This makes no sense or encourage individuals to make positive change.

A Learning Culture

Having a vocal executive champion and empowered and engaged employees will have little impact unless there is a culture where improvement is expected. There needs to be an expectation that the organization learns and grows.

A key aspect of driving a learning culture where continuous improvement is the norm, is fostering a culture of collaboration. It is the one big issue that virtually all businesses face, that is, functional barriers that prevent effective working.

All businesses to a greater or lesser extent are siloed. You may feel as a senior leader you are in lockstep with your peers, but as you move down through the management layers, few organizations manifest themselves with the same commitment as vocalized around the top table. Your role as a leader is to break down barriers and encourage employees to work collaboratively throughout the organization toward shared goals.

In some organizations, quality is seen as the responsibility of the Quality team. This is clearly contrary to the establishment of a true culture of quality. In reality, quality is everybody's concern and needs everybody's involvement.

You need to drive cross-functional collaboration. For example, Manufacturing and Quality are working together to resolve quality issues in manufacturing. Again, good examples are where the leaders accountable for those groups are seen closely collaborating and working together. Leading by example and demonstrating that a common objective is shared will help set the tone for establishing a culture of quality.

Practical ways also include cross-functional representation at all key meetings down throughout the business and, as we covered, that your Quality team is embedded physically with its peer functions.

The Quality function may not have a completely servant relationship with other functions, as at times it needs to give honest and candid feedback as only a valued colleague can. But it does need to be there to support and help. Your role as a leader is to ensure that everything is in place to facilitate this effective dialogue.

Much of this book has been focused on ways to shape the Quality group to better plan, implement, and facilitate the QMS. It is, however, not possible for the Quality organization to do all of this completely "in-house." Other functions have key accountabilities and responsibilities in ensuring that the quality system works effectively. A key part of your role as a leader is to articulate the role of the QMS more widely, such that all functions needed for success are on the same page. As we will cover shortly, the Quality unit plays a vital role in educating, coaching, and mentoring the wider business in the role of the quality system and importance of quality, though in practice this does not always happen.

Many organizations have integrated lean approaches such as "Gemba" walks with senior leadership walking the production floor and engaging with employees. There is also often an expectation that continuous improvement is visible on the shopfloor, with a board detailing projects and savings.

Let's be honest, many such exercises are no more than show. Many times, these endeavors are not the result of a restless dissatisfaction with the status quo, which is the culture we want to create, but political performances as functional leaders and their reports align behind what is expected of them when the senior management team arrive. A key question for you is: would these projects have happened if I wasn't visiting the area?

Similarly, the object of the exercise in many Operational Excellence programs is to attain certification in Six Sigma or lean, and once the qualification is attained the skills are rarely used again.

A key aspect in making such approaches more than just show is articulating to your staff the Why? It is vital for all improvement of the QMS that the output to be directly related to something that the customer deems important. This should drive true performance metrics.

Several years ago, a major U.S. department store performed an exercise asking their shop assistants what they considered to be the primary purpose of their jobs. Surprisingly, the majority answered that the main reason for coming to work was to prevent customers stealing from the store. This obviously created and encouraged very specific behaviors, ones not necessarily aligned with selling clothes to the public in a friendly manner. Likewise, you have a huge influence on your organization's behaviors by the things you deem important.

If you have an operational unit whose performance is solely judged on delivery, then this is what you will get. Similarly, if you have a Quality organization that is solely judged on compliance, then that is what you will get. You need to articulate the wider goals and why these matter for a learning culture to be of any use.

The What and When?—Planning a Quality Transformation

In the next section, we will lay out the steps needed to construct your T-map. Like all the maps they are useless if you don't know where you want to go or have little understanding of where you are.

As an introduction, the concepts we will cover work equally well at the departmental as well as the enterprise level. This model has been built over 20 years of continually deploying and refining this approach in a range of organizations. We have tested the approach in multiple environments, all with their own unique challenges and opportunities. Along the way there have been many learnings that we will share, so hopefully you will avoid the pitfalls and errors we have made.

In truth, the process we describe is not novel. We have, however, brought together aspects of several established methodologies based on what works contingent to specific situations. We have found force fitting any one approach blindly does not work.

Components of a Quality Organization Transformation

There are several elements that form part of a Quality Transformation. Some elements are shared and involve the broader organization, while others are not. Figure 8.1 describes these elements, which we will cover in turn.

Feedback

You're going to need to get feedback, horizontally and vertically throughout the organization. This may be in the form of one-to-one interviews or it may be in the form of surveys, collective group discussions, or seeking

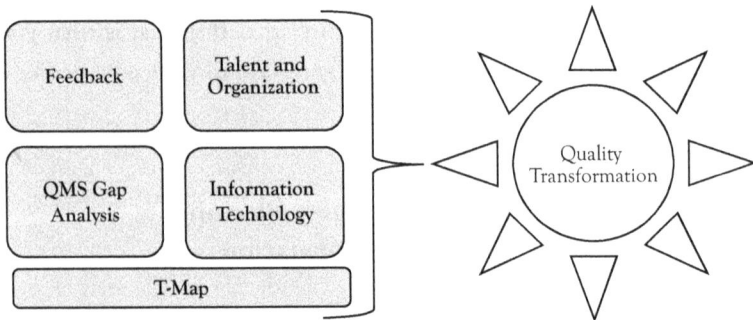

Figure 8.1 Elements of a quality transformation

out external opinion. The prime purpose at this stage is to gain understanding of the opinion of your workforce regarding quality and the quality system. What in the QMS is holding them back? What change is needed for them to be more successful as a business unit or an individual within your organization?

In many businesses, the process of understanding is a challenging exercise with many business partners venting their frustration at what they see as the bureaucratic and complex processes inflicted on them by their Quality unit. You may need to brace yourself. To get the best out of these exchanges you need to listen. This requires a certain level of endurance; however, the insight you will gain will be invaluable in understanding what needs to change.

We recommend that you interview at least 10 percent of the total workforce or at least 50 people ensuring that you connect with *all* the major functions within the business, even those you would rarely work with.

An effective way to structure the interview is around the following questions:

- What's working?
- What's not working?
- What's missing/holding you back?

Start with explaining that you are seeking to understand ways in which the Quality function can better serve the needs of the business. Explain that you need honest and open feedback for this exercise to be meaningful and help create a strategic plan of change. This stage is all about understanding views. Make sure you take copious notes or ideally record interviews where possible. You will not be attempting to fix everybody's specific grievances, but rather better understand people's concerns.

It is tempting to use online surveys, as these can have greater reach. Constructing an effective survey is a key skill and a poorly designed survey can, at best, confuse and, at worst, generate an incorrect conclusion. In addition, in creating a survey it is very tempting for those within the Quality organization to focus on surveys that are quantitative in nature: on a scale of 1 to 10 and so on. However, feedback that is narrative is often more valuable. You are likely to hear: "my view of the quality system is…." This qualitative data is equally as valid as objective, analytical data that you can draw a graph with. If you are going down the survey route it is well worth consulting some of the material on creating effective surveys that is available, before using this medium to gain understanding [58].

While surveys have value, in our experience there is no substitute for an in-depth, face-to-face candid discussion. Surveys miss out on key elements for long-term success that is, building relationships and personal support for the transformation. Building trust is something that should not be overlooked, and you may have to invest time building relationships before expecting to be provided with frank, open feedback. This is especially true if you are relatively new to the organization.

The next stage of the process is organizing the feedback based on key themes and areas of opportunity or improvement. At this stage, do not share widely, it may still be too early to communicate plans or even insights. Share your initial analysis report with your executive leadership, seek their perspective.

Key learnings from our experience include:

- Despite what you hear—check facts before coming to any firm conclusions.
- This is a critical decision point in the process; this is the first "go/no-go" decision point for your transformation. You may decide after initial analysis that you can achieve your objectives via other means.
- Be cognizant that in your position as a business leader, individuals will often tell you things that they think you want to hear. Do not be scared to keep asking: why is that?

Talent and Organizational Review

From the feedback exercise you will get a sense of whether your Quality organization is supporting the business. It will come back to the same three questions from both the feedback and the T-Map exercise: What's working? What's not working? And What's missing?

However, a more sensitive issue is whether, or not, your current staff are delivering. In this case, the questions become:

- Who's contributing?
- Who's not contributing (and why)?
- Who's missing?

Great care is obviously needed in soliciting this type of feedback. You should not ask these questions as part of the feedback survey, and certainly not as part of the T-Map exercise. But they are questions you will need to ask yourself in reviewing the capability of your Quality organization.

You may discover that there are skill sets or experience that are missing and this will require a recruitment or training plan. Consider skills that you need now, as well as competencies that you will need in the future based on the guidance in the previous chapter.

The aim of this step is to assess overall capability and its ability to service the customer and organization. A good guide to such analysis can be found in *Good to Great* by Jim Collins where forming the right team is vital to success [50]. One of the key insights that Collins espoused was that the team needs to be in place *before* starting the transformation. Our experience agrees with this. Having the right Quality team with the right players in place ensures a consistent approach during what will be a period of significant change.

Also look at staffing levels with the aim to achieve an approximate ratio of Quality staff to total workforce of approximately 10 percent. This ratio will depend heavily on your product portfolio, type of industry, and overall business model and maturity.

In addition, review span of control ensuring that staff have roles that they can both deliver and have a sense of ownership. Related to the last point, review critical business relationships, and ensure that stakeholders units have access to a dedicated Quality resource.

In essence, you should identify either key partnerships or processes and align your Quality organization specific to the needs of your business.

Based on our experience in the medical device industry, Figure 8.2 describes a typical organizational design. In smaller organizations, the quality team may have people playing all or combinations of these roles.

Key Business Partner		Quality Team	Key Accountabilities
Manufacturing	⬌	Quality Operations	Manufacturing support, validation, product release
Research and Development	⬌	Design Quality	Design and development process
Procurement	⬌	Supplier Quality	Supplier performance, raw material sourcing
Cross functional (HR, IT etc.)	⬌	Quality Systems	Development of the quality system, internal audit
Sales and Marketing	⬌	Commercial Quality	Sales and marketing of offering
Customer support	⬌	Complaint Handling Unit	Complaints and field actions; customer support

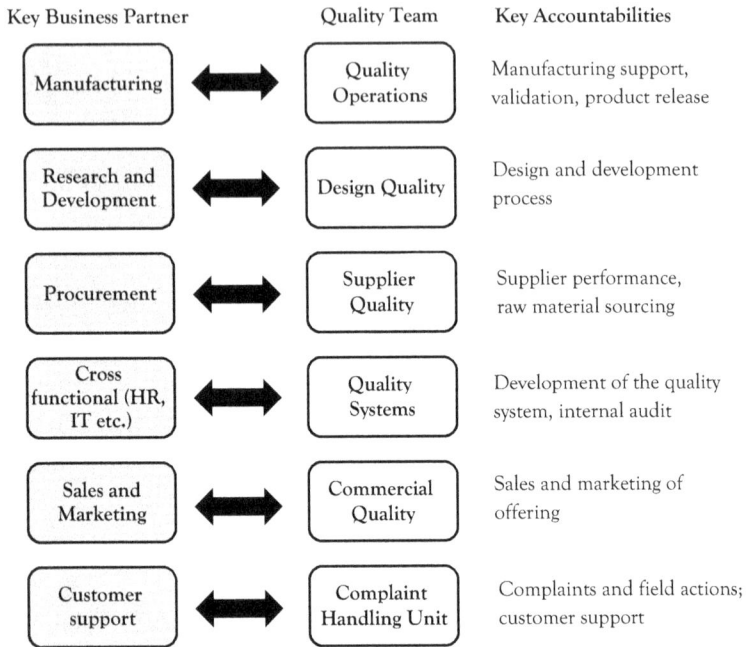

Figure 8.2 Quality teams, their accountabilities, and appropriate business partners

This is a critical aspect of transforming a company's Quality culture and building a solid foundation for the transformation. Both are dependent on relationships. Having dedicated teams forms strong bonds between Quality and business units. This is equally true for external relationships, for example, regional/country teams, suppliers, clients, and so on.

Compare and contrast this to two scenarios we have often observed. First, one where the Quality unit has a solely compliance-focused interface with the business. In essence, the Quality unit has a policing role with obvious consequences for its ongoing relationship with its business partners. Or secondly, the Quality unit has the bulk of their interaction with the organization at the end of the manufacturing process or during the tail-end of a project, in a review/approve capacity. In this scenario, the business runs a serious risk of significantly increased work in progress or project delays due to both capacity within the Quality group and any tendency for the unit to take an overly policing role regarding documentation quality. Often, more energy is expended as documents are reworked, rather than invested in efforts to implement corrective action to improve document quality in the longer term.

In the model proposed, Quality is integrated with its business partners throughout the extended supply chain and associated business units. For many organizations this really is a paradigm change in the role of the Quality function, but for the business to be successful Quality needs to be involved throughout the life cycle of the project, process, or product. They need to be involved at the outset when specifications, criteria, or objectives are agreed upon.

This may seem obvious, but it is surprising the number of organizations that miss this practical and beneficial approach. This model does require that the roles and accountabilities of each team within Quality are clear by all. Ensure that you have some form of RACI document (Responsible, Accountable, Consult, Inform) not only for the Quality teams, but your business partners as well. Significant time is lost, and expense incurred when roles and responsibilities are not clear.

Conversely, it also requires that a degree of common sense is applied and the demarcation between Quality groups isn't taken to an extreme and teams are able to flex to support peaks in demand. While there is a level of specialism within each team, there should also be "bread-and-butter" activities that any individual in any Quality team should have the competence to cover.

Regarding the practicalities of the location of the Quality unit, there are numerous inefficiencies generated when Quality units are physically separated from the groups they are supporting. Examples have been seen where they are on different floors, or even separate buildings, and communicate solely via e-mail. This does not aid the collaboration that we are seeking.

In moving a Quality team to sit physically with their business partner, direct contact, discussion, and ultimately a mutual coaching environment is created. This builds teamwork and ultimately leads to shared objectives and metrics. There are obviously scenarios where Quality units can support remotely in this highly interconnected Internet world, but do not forget the power of bringing groups together where correct and swift decisions need to be made. But beware, an individual's work environment is very personal. Do not underestimate the resistance you may encounter in moving individuals away from their physical domains of influence, but such challenges can be overcome and are outweighed by the significant benefits to the business in doing so.

One by-product of bringing collaborative teams together in situ is processes that are often executed sequentially, for example approval of documentation, decision making, and so on, can now be executed either in parallel or simultaneously. Examples include approval of validation reports, creation of change control plans, or completion of other quality records such as nonconformances and corrective action plans. This vastly increases the flexibility and speed with which these documents can be generated if you bring together individuals that usually operate sequentially. In addition, its benefits also include improved compliance, documentation quality, and increases the knowledge and capability of all involved.

Key learnings from our experience include:

- Have your organizational design set and in place before starting the T-Map.
- Changing your organization mid-transformation will disrupt the implementation.
- Make changes quickly and comprehensively.

Quality System Gap Analysis

Following the approaches described above you will quickly discover pain points in the quality system and organization. It is important that you do not dilly-dally in addressing concerns, especially concerns that can be easily fixed. Look for and deliver quick wins. This is important as it not only starts improving the system but it also signals that you are listening to concerns and gives the transformation process credibility.

One vital—and obvious—point to make is that despite all the content in this book about improving the efficiency, usability, and positioning the quality system to meet multiple customer groups, it still *must* be fully compliant. Any changes that you implement through the guidance in this book still need to be looked at through the lens of the regulations applying to your industry.

This next step in the transformation involves a comprehensive and thorough gap assessment to understand the level of compliance with all the regulations and standards that apply to you. It consists of going through the requirement of each regulation or standard and assessing whether your Quality system can meet this requirement. Include input from recent external and internal audits/inspections and if needed bring in external expertise if you feel this activity cannot be executed in-house.

If your QMS is mature, it is unlikely that you will identify areas that are deemed critical. However, you will not be certain until you complete the exercise. This is especially true for organizations that are relatively new, or you have little experience of. Areas that are deemed critical need to be addressed at once. Appropriate RCA, correction and corrective action needs to be applied, and the issue fast-tracked through your change process.

Importantly, you *must* explain to the organization the value of *self*-identifying compliance gaps. If there are noncompliant aspects of the QMS that individuals are already aware of, now is the time to put up their hands such that it can be remedied. You would rather self-identify and be masters of your own destiny, than have the issue being found during a potentially painful regulatory inspection. However, team leaders and managers of areas may be reluctant to expose deficiencies in their own areas. You may need to come up with creative ways so that these compliance gaps can be flushed out. For example, bringing in neutral, external assessors or create ways for compliance gaps to be raised in confidence.

As with all audits, this exercise is only based on looking at a sample to predict the overall population. It is better to do a larger and more statistically valid sample and come to the appropriate decision, than to look at a smaller number of records and be inappropriately reassured of your compliance position. We recommend approximately 20 percent of each quality record type, for example nonconformance, batch-record, and so on, be reviewed to determine which category you place each quality system element in. This is not a quick exercise but is a critical part in the quality transformation.

Key learnings from our experience include:

- Ensure the executive and the organization understands the risks of noncompliance and why it is a vital part of the transformation.

Information Technology

The role of information technology (IT) is now central to the management of quality in most businesses. It is core to supporting information sharing and generating an efficient operation. With increasing levels of automation and testing across the supply chain, the ability to harvest, organize, and visualize significant amounts of interconnected data is now central to making sound decisions.

As discussed earlier, if you are using paper to manage your quality system you will need a strategy to invest in an IT solution for managing quality. If you already have an e-QMS solution, you should review it thoroughly for workflow efficiency and its ability to provide process and product performance insight. Again, look at such system through the eyes of waste reduction and the ability to help you make better decisions as covered in previous chapters.

If the tools you are using to manage your quality system are a source of frustration, you will certainly hear it in the feedback and the T-Map session. You will have to decide whether to develop what you have currently or invest in an alternative solution. There are already great solutions out there. With a variety of cloud-based, Software as a Service—SaaS— solutions now commercially available, there is little in the way preventing you accessing software offering industry standard, if not best, practice.

The object here is to avoid reinventing the wheel and to access solutions developed in partnership with customers like you. Customization of the IT solution is to be avoided. It is preferable to find a product with a workflow that you can use and deploy with zero customization and minimal configuration.

Key learnings from our experience include:

- A new IT tool will not be the transformation in itself. If the culture of quality doesn't change then the outcome will be the same, just with a different IT solution.

- Do not allow a quality transformation to be confused with technology deployment.
- Involve users from all areas when deploying an e-QMS.

Building Your Quality Transformation Map

A T-Map is a deceptively simple tool that can describe the strategic journey of an organization from current to desired future state over a medium-term timeframe—typically three to five years. It is usually a one-page visual description of the steps necessary to execute a strategic transformation. More than anything, it is a communication and engagement tool to show how multiple change elements are united in realizing a better future state for the organization.

To be successful, T-Maps need to be created by a broad cross-functional team representing different perspectives within—and sometimes from outside—the business unit. This ensures that the future state benefits the overall organization and not an individual department or section. This can sometimes be an uncomfortable exercise with truths, known and unknown, being revealed.

It is important to state that often you may not be able to identify the appropriate fixes for certain issues. You need to create an appropriate placeholder for further RCA when appropriate. This does not negate performing further investigational work to gain understanding when needed.

Conversely, it is critical that you are pragmatic where there are obvious solutions that need to be applied. For example, if your document management system is paper-based, cumbersome, and bureaucratic, identifying a project to address this does not need to be preceded by an extensive 5 Whys activity to determine why it is outdated. Again, use the methodology with common sense and only use it when it helps.

It is critical that before you start to create the T-Map that you have secured executive sponsorship. It is highly likely that you will need to secure their ongoing support and resources to ensure the T-Map will deliver against its goals.

Regarding the practicalities of executing a T-Map exercise, you will need a skilled facilitator; a cross-functional team—ideally no less than 10 and no more than 20 people and a large venue with plenty of wall space. With respect to how many sessions to hold, it may be preferable to hold multiple sessions and aggregate these exercises. This will certainly be necessary if your business has multiple locations. Ideally, run the sessions with staff not involved in the initial feedback exercise, to get input from a broader selection of staff. In addition, we have found that though remote interactive sessions can be more effort to execute, they can be effective. Figure 8.3 covers the main stages of the T-map building exercise.

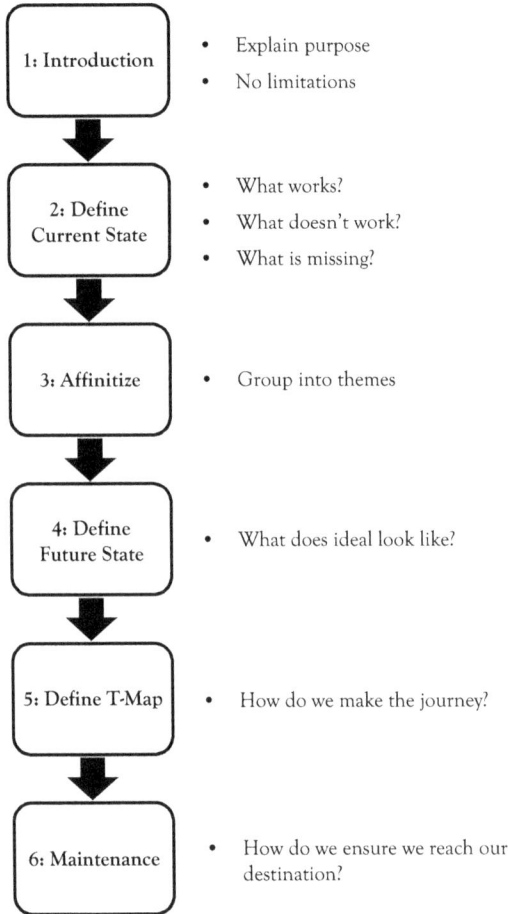

1: Introduction
- Explain purpose
- No limitations

2: Define Current State
- What works?
- What doesn't work?
- What is missing?

3: Affinitize
- Group into themes

4: Define Future State
- What does ideal look like?

5: Define T-Map
- How do we make the journey?

6: Maintenance
- How do we ensure we reach our destination?

Figure 8.3 Creating your quality transformation map

Step 1: Introduction

This should last no more than 30 minutes and should cover the purpose of the session. The general ground-rules for any brainstorming activity apply.

Step 2: Define the Current State (30–60 min)

This session covers the current "as is" state. You normally contain the scope to focus the session, for example: what is it like to use the QMS? The key questions to ask are as follows:

- What works?
- What doesn't work?
- What is missing?

Have the participants write their comments down on sticky notes and put them up on a wall. If you can use a color-coded system for the questions above, you will easily see the balance between positive and negative comments. When you see that the production of comments is starting to slow, pull the team together and provide them with 15 minutes or so to review all the comments. Ask if there are any comments that anyone would like to highlight as interesting or that need additional clarity.

Step 3: Affinitize (30–45 mins)

This step comprises of collecting the comments into common groups, which usually begin to form 5 to 10 key categories. Ask the team to comment on the key categories—were there any surprises or key insights/ learning points? What were some of the themes within the categories? Note these, as they will be used in the construction of the T-Map.

Step 4: Define Future State (30–60 minutes)

For each of the key categories, ask the team to define what "ideal" would look like. Again, use sticky notes to capture thoughts and ideas. It is recommended that you organize the wall so that current and future state notes are relative to each other, with space in between for the final step. Ask the team to comment on the future state comments—were there any surprises or key insights/learning points? What were some of the common themes? Note these, as they will be used in the construction of the T-Map.

Step 5: Defining the Transformation Map (60–90 mins)

This final step is the one that requires the undivided attention of a skilled facilitator. The key question to ask here is: how can you make the journey from current state to future state? Other questions include:

- What capabilities, systems, and processes need to be changed or put in place to achieve the future state?
- Is there a sequence of actions or projects that need to be completed or can a parallel track approach be used?
- What level of investment will you need?
- Can your transformation be realistically delivered in your timeframe?

Once the steps have been identified, they should be plotted onto a T-Map template—there are hard copy templates and app/software solutions available widely on the Internet.

The T-Map can be included as part of your organization's QSMR to show the mid- to long-term strategic plan as part of the Quality Planning process. KPIs/metrics critical to demonstrate progress against the plan and to show the impact it is having on business performance should also be considered.

Figure 8.4 shows an example T-Map showing high-level summary descriptions of the current state assessment in the left and bottom axes. In the top right-hand corner are high-level summary descriptions of the desired future state. The paths from current to future state are split according to the key categories identified in Steps 3 to 4. The progression from current to future state is then defined by the actions/projects identified in Step 5.

Quality Transformation Map

Current State	Year 1	Year 2	Year 3	Future State
Complex Procedures	Improve Raw Material CTQs	Reduce Muda in Change Control Process	Implement Annual Product Lifecycle Reviews	Class Leading Compliance / Industry 4.0
Quality Reviews at End of Process	Implement Quality Planning Process	Improve Data Trending	Implement Supplier Score Cards	eQMS ERP Data Sharing
	Create Site Master Plan	Implement Enhanced Systemic Analysis in QSMR	Build Cost of Quality Model	Implement LIMS
Processes	Reduce Muda in NC, RCI & CAPA Processes	Reduce Validation Deviations	Implement Comprehensive Training and Development Program	Improved Speed to Market
Compliance Issues	Engage QARA Teams at Project or Change Outset		Co-Locate QE Teams with Operations and R&D Teams	QARA Is A Business Asset
Poor Connectivity Between QMS Sub Processes	Undertake QARA Organizational Review (Capacity & Capability)		Drive Accountability & Reduce Numbers of Document Approvers	QARA Experience Secondments / Complete IVDR Transition
No QMS Development Plan			Create QARA RACI and Assign Business Partner Leads	Complete Mitigation Of QMS Gaps
	Create 3 Year Resource & Hiring Plan			Deliver Audit Training
QARA Teams Not Aligned to Business Partners	Deliver Regulatory Awareness Training for All Staff		Implement Effective QS KPIs	Complete REACH Product Updates / Create Data Lakes
QARA Perceived As Bureaucratic	No Compliance Lead	Define Training Plans for Key Roles	Redefine Internal Audit Program	Implement EBR
Insufficient QARA Knowledge Across the Business	No Defined Training Plan for Key Roles	Undertake QMS Gap Analysis	Assign Clear QMS Sub System Ownership	Publish QARA KPI Dashboards
Insufficient QA Resources	No RACI			Implement eQMS
		Compliance Issues	Complex Internal Audit Plan	Zero Connectivity Between Systems / No eSignatures
		No QS Design		
		IVDR Readiness	Audit Readiness	Paper Based Systems / Limited Systemic Analysis

People **Compliance** **Technology**

Figure 8.4 An example of a quality transformation map

The actions/projects are typically sequenced so that an evolving strategy of improvement is deployed. This will be dictated by priorities, capabilities, budgets, and so on, with dependencies linking key improvements following one after the other. One distinct advantage of the T-Map is that by using a cross-functional team that represents the life cycle of your processes and products, you are simultaneously incorporating both systems and a degree of complexity-based thinking into the analysis.

Step 6: Maintenance of the Transformation Map

The T-Map is—more than anything else—a communication tool. It should be reviewed regularly with the entire organization to show how the strategy is progressing. You should be clear in highlighting completed steps and how the next steps are either in the planning phase or already in execution.

However, it needs to be a flexible tool. Even with a relatively short strategic horizon, situations and environment can change, and the T-Map should not be religiously adhered to. If changes are necessary to adapt the strategy for example, delete actions/projects that no longer make sense or the addition of new ones, then these should be updated following consultation with your stakeholders/sponsors.

The Future State objectives rarely change but the means to get there will, as the business and environment evolves. In over 20 years of using T-Maps to drive strategic transformations, the authors have never completed a transformation with the same T-Map they started with.

In summary, revise your T-Map regularly but your Future State objectives should not change. If the T-Map is reviewed regularly to communicate progress, it will build credibility within the organization and affirm that the skills, behaviors, and ways of working that the organization has identified for the future state are something that the workforce can believe in. If it is sustained over the stated timeframe, the use of T-Map will drive lasting, beneficial, and meaningful change.

Key learnings from our experience include:

- The T-Map as a communication tool: don't underestimate the importance of showing progress (remind the organization where you started and where you are heading).

- The cross-functional team will naturally incorporate systems and complexity based thinking and, as a result, the T-Map will create a comprehensive program of change.
- Most organizations have three main types of people with views on change: The Evangelist, the Team Player, and the Doubting Thomas. When selecting people to be involved, make sure you include representatives from all three groups. The Doubting Thomas can often be (a) source of truth, (b) reality checks, and (c) often turns into an Evangelist when they see their views are being heeded.
- Some T-Map changes (e.g., changing your CAPA process) will be projects in their own right; in these cases, we recommend you implement individual project plans and track progress closely. Others (e.g., increasing headcount in a particular team) will just require management decision and action.

The How?—Goals, Training, and Recognition

The above sections should help in your endeavor in creating a culture of quality—the Why—and build a plan covering what you need to have in place to transform your organization—the What and When.

It won't tell you *How* to make change happen.

As a Quality leader you're not going to do all of this yourself. It's going to have to happen through those you are responsible for. This is easier said than done and is one of the main challenges of leadership that is, getting stuff to happen through other people.

To make the quality transformation reality, you are going to have to pull several levers. Essentially it comprises three components:

- Setting goals and objectives
- Providing training and support
- Recognizing and rewarding success

Goals and Objectives

You are going to have to work with the business and to find appropriate goals whose completion will help drive your transformation. These need to be incorporated into everybody's specific goals and objectives.

In addition, if you want to foster an environment of cross-functional and within-team collaboration, you are going to have to set shared goals to drive cooperative working. You will need to define KPIs that truly measure success, following some of the guidance in previous chapters.

Similarly, your role as a leader is not to develop, implement, or even identify solutions. Your job is to create appropriate goals and give the organization the appropriate tools and training to solve these problems themselves. While it may be very tempting for you to roll up your sleeves, you need to allow your organization to rise to the challenges you are setting and solve these problems themselves. This can be an issue for some leaders, who may not exhibit the degree of humility needed to understand that they themselves do not have all the answers, or even know all the appropriate questions to ask. Your job is to facilitate the process and help break down barriers in the way.

Training and Support

Training takes many forms. The way you behave as a leader and the things that you tolerate, and those you will not tolerate are also a form of training for your organization. The behaviors you exhibit daily are no less powerful than formal classroom training and form the vehicle by which you tell your organization the issues you consider to be important and start setting the social norms within your business.

Social norms are generally established during our upbringing and are, in essence, a form of training. The more established the social norm, the harder it is to change to a new set of beliefs. This may be a challenge if you inherit a business with a culture of quality distant from the one you want.

Training establishes a consistent set of behaviors. Behaviors are then the foundation of culture. Training, therefore, is fundamental to creating the culture you want to establish. In practice, this means a significant, dedicated, and focused effort, sustained over a period of years to ensure that a culture is established and remains in place.

The trend in delivering training via "virtual" methods has grown over recent years. Many organizations now rely on videos or slide decks containing animations to deliver their training. In our experience, this is no better than the basic "read and understand."

The issue with all training is that different people interpret information in different ways, executing their own beliefs and scripts as covered previously. This leads to inconsistency in execution of the quality system. At times, this is potentially dangerous. When making certain products, there are certain activities that must be performed correctly each time. Such activities should be automated or extensively error proofed rather than relying on interpretation by individuals. For other areas that aren't so critical, the temptation can be to put exquisite detail within the documentation to explain what is needed. The drawback is such an approach can generate significant compliance challenges, as individuals struggle to comply with sometimes contradictory instructions.

One of the key messages within this book is that to work in the Quality organization it means working in a world that isn't black and white. It is a gray world. Judgments are made based on experience, wisdom, and balance of risk. In many cases, it is impossible to document every single scenario within a given procedure.

This is the nub of the role of the Quality professional: bringing balanced judgment and helping business partners interpret and execute the quality system effectively and efficiently. In our experience, there is no substitute for effective classroom training and one-to-one coaching/mentoring in the workplace. While requiring more effort, classroom training allows rich discussion and, importantly, assessment of the learning needed to truly embed knowledge, skills, and competencies.

From your analysis of your organizational needs, you will identify key training themes that need addressing. Some of these may be related to specific aspects of the quality system, others may be technical, and others may be softer and more behavioral in nature. Addressing these training gaps via subject matter expert led sessions will yield faster and more comprehensive improvements and will ultimately lead to the desired behaviors becoming adopted.

Reward and Recognition

Giving individuals appropriate goals, training and then hoping a transformational change will happen may work as a one-time activity, but it will not be sustainable. You as a leader need to recognize and reward achievements and continually encourage your organization on its journey, a journey that will have several successes and failures along the way.

Firstly, you need to understand there must be some degree of reward and recognition, even if it is as small as thanking individuals for their efforts and articulating how their efforts are making a difference. Secondly, whichever program you have in place, be it awards, performance related pay or yearly bonuses, you need to make sure that it drives the behaviors you want to see that is, customer focus, continuous improvement, collaborative working, and effective management of risk. Systems that rely on an individual's bonuses being linked to completion of individual specific goals in our experience can drive quite focused thinking and behaviors not always consistent with those you want to see.

Final Thoughts

Throughout this book we have covered many aspects. We have reviewed the role of quality and Quality organizations and articulated our view that these should be repositioned in some organizations. It could be argued this stance is more aligned with previous approaches to quality management such as TQM.

We have covered the need of the QMS to support different customer groups and the role of change and risk management in shaping the effectiveness, efficiency, and adequacy of the quality system.

We have also reviewed some of the newer aspects around systems thinking and viewing quality organizations as complex adaptive systems and how such approaches can aid decision making and be more reflective of how organizations really function today. We have covered the importance of situational analysis to identify the best response and effectively balance the needs of innovation and control. The influence of these aspects on practical organizational design that is, process, people, and technology has also been reviewed with current and future challenges in mind.

In this final chapter, we have attempted to cover more practical aspects of Quality organizational transformation based on our years of experience performing such activities within a range of small and large companies with significant measurable success.

In many respects, the approach and scenarios detailed in the material is a best case. Some organizations have greater challenges than others, some less, and importantly there is no "one size that fits all." As covered previously, applying a methodology and rigidly treating organizations as machines has not always been successful. While allowing the system to run free is also neither advantageous for the business or the end customer.

The approaches we have articulated generally sit in the middle ground between rigid control and complete freedom. Though bizarrely there are also situations where taking these extreme approaches may be the best option. While such guidance may not be as clearly defined and prescriptive as some business leaders would want, this is the reality of the world we inhabit.

We hope some of the guidance in the book will be useful, on both a theoretical and practical level.

If you work in Quality, you have our absolute respect. It is a world that is challenging, frustrating, appears thankless at times, and one that is, ultimately, absolutely rewarding.

References

1. International Consortium of Investigative Journalists. November 25, 2018. "Medical Devices Harm Patients Worldwide as Governments Fail on Safety." icij .org. www.icij.org/investigations/implant-files/medical-devices-harm-patients-worldwide-as-governments-fail-on-safety/.

2. Garvin, D.A. November 1987. "Competing on the Eight Dimensions of Quality." *Harvard Business Review*. hbr.org. https://hbr.org/1987/11/competing-on-the-eight-dimensions-of-quality.

3. Fuhr, T., K. George, and J. Pai. October 2013. "The Business Case for Medical Device Quality." mckinsey.com. www.mckinsey.com/~/media/mckinsey/dotcom/client_service/public%20sector/regulatory%20excellence/the_business_case_for_medical_device_quality.ashx.

4. International Standards Organization. June 2022. "ISO13485:2016, Medical Devices—Quality Management Systems—Requirements for Regulatory Purposes." iso.org. www.iso.org/standard/59752.html.

5. Protard, M. and R. Lough. May 2020. "French Court Orders Damages for Victims of PIP Breast Implant Scandal." reuters.com. www.reuters.com/world/europe/french-court-victims-pip-breast-implant-scandal-should-be-compensated-2021-05-20/.

6. Reuters staff. October 2019. "Johnson & Johnson Agrees to Pay About $117 Million to Settle U.S. States' Mesh Probe." reuters.com. www.reuters.com/article/us-johnson-johnson-settlement-mesh-idUSKBN1WW2EK.

7. Reuters staff. May 2019. "J&J Agrees to Pay About $1 Billion to Resolve Hip Implant Lawsuits: Bloomberg." reuters.com. www.reuters.com/article/us-johnson-johnson-settlement-idUSKCN1SD1YO.

8. Food and Drug Administration. June 2022. "CFR—Code of Federal Regulations Title 2: Quality System Regulations." accessdata.fda.gov. www.accessdata.fda.gov/scripts/cdrh/cfdocs/cfcfr/CFRSearch.cfm?CFRPart=820.

9. US Food and Drug Administration. December 16, 2021. "2021 Medical Device Recalls." fda.gov. www.fda.gov/medical-devices/medical-device-recalls/2021-medical-device-recalls.

10. Brown, A., J. Eatock, D. Dixon, B. Meenan, and J. Anderson. 2008. "Quality and Continuous Improvement in Medical Device Manufacturing." *The TQM Journal* 20, no. 6, pp. 541–555. http://dx.doi.org/10.1108/17542730810909329.

11. Drucker, P.F. 2012. *Management Challenges for the 21st Century*, 1st ed. Taylor and Francis. www.perlego.com/book/1621689/management-challenges-for-the-21st-century-pdf.

12. Kotter, J.P. January 1995. "Leading Change: Why Transformation Efforts Fail." *Harvard Business Review*. hbr.org. https://hbr.org/1995/05/leading-change-why-transformation-efforts-fail-2.

13. Nasim, S. and Sushil. 2011. "Revisiting Organizational Change: Exploring the Paradox of Managing Continuity and Change." *Journal of Change Management* 11, no. 2,pp. 185–206. https://doi.org/10.1080/14697017.2010.538854.

14. Duphily, R.J. May 2014. "Root Cause Investigation Best Practice Guide: Aerospace Report No. TOR-2014-02202." The Aerospace Corporation. apps.dtic.mil. https://apps.dtic.mil/sti/pdfs/ADA626691.pdf.

15. Ognibene, S. and I. Binnie. February 2015. "Costa Concordia Captain Sentenced to 16 Years for 2012 Shipwreck." reuters.com. www.reuters.com/article/us-italy-ship-idUSKBN0LF12H20150211.

16. Robson, D. 2020. *The Intelligence Trap*. London: Hodder & Stoughton.

17. Tinsley, C.H., R.L. Dillon, and P.M. Madsen. April 2011. "How to Avoid Catastrophe." *Harvard Business Review*. hbr.org. https://hbr.org/2011/04/how-to-avoid-catastrophe.

18. Tinsley, C.H., R.L. Dillon, and M.A. Cronin. 2012. "How Near-Miss Events Amplify or Attenuate Risky Decision Making." *Management Science* 58, no. 9, pp. 1596–1613. https://doi.org/10.1287/mnsc.1120.1517.

19. National Commission on the BP Deepwater Horizon Oil Spill and Offshore Drilling. January 2011. "Deep Water: The Gulf Oil Disaster and the Future of Offshore Drilling." govinfo.gov. www.govinfo.gov/content/pkg/GPO-OILCOMMISSION/pdf/GPO-OILCOMMISSION.pdf.

20. Edmondson, A.C. April 2011. "Strategies for Learning From Failure." hbr.org. *Harvard Business Review*. https://hbr.org/2011/04/strategies-for-learning-from-failure.

21. Øgland, P. 2008. "Designing Quality Management Systems as Complex Adaptive systems." *Systemist* 30, no. 3, pp. 468–491.

22. World Health Organization. 2009. "Systems Thinking for Health Systems Strengthening." D. de Savigny and T. Adam, eds. www.who.int. https://apps.who.int/iris/bitstream/handle/10665/44204/9789241563895_eng.pdf?sequence=1&isAllowed=y.

23. US Food & Drug Administration. March 24, 2021. "FDA Opioid Systems Modelling Effort." fda.gov. www.fda.gov/drugs/information-drug-class/fda-opioid-systems-modeling-effort.

24. Bradley, D.T., M.A. Mansouria, F. Keea, and L.M.T. Garcia. 2020. "A Systems Approach to Preventing and Responding to COVID-19." *Clinical Medicine* 21, p. 100325. https://doi.org/10.1016/j.eclinm.2020.100325.

25. Seddon, J. 2003. *Freedom From Command and Control*. Vanguard Consulting Ltd. www.beyondcommandandcontrol.com.

26. Leape, L.L. 1997. "A Systems Analysis Approach to Medical Error." *Journal of Evaluation in Clinical Practice* 3, no. 3, pp. 213–222. https://doi.org/10.1046/j.1365-2753.1997.00006.x.

27. Reason, J.T. 1997. *Managing the Risks of Organizational Accidents*. Aldershot, Hampshire, England: Ashgate Publishing Ltd.

28. Shaw, J., R. Taylor, and K. Dix. 2015. "Uses and Abuses of Performance Data in Healthcare." Dr Foster. www.drfoster.com. www.patientlibrary.net/tempgen/29702.pdf.

29. Jones, P. and K. Schimanski. 2010. "The Four Hour Target to Reduce Emergency Department 'Waiting Time': A Systematic Review of Clinical Outcomes." *Emergency Medicine Australasia* 22, no. 5, pp. 391–398. https://doi.org/10.1111/j.1742-6723.2010.01330.x.

30. Boulton, J.G., P.M. Allen, and C. Bowman. 2015. *Embracing Complexity: Strategic Perspectives for an Age of Turbulence*. Oxford University Press.

31. Snowden, D.J. and M.E. Boone. November 2007. "A Leader's Framework for Decision Making." *Harvard Business Review*. hbr.org.

32. Snowden, D. and A. Rancati. 2021. "Managing Complexity (and Chaos) in Times of Crisis. A Field Guide for Decision Makers Inspired by the Cynefin Framework." Luxembourg: Publications Office of the European Union. https://publications.jrc.ec.europa.eu/repository/handle/JRC123629.

33. Streatfield, P. 2001. *The Paradox of Control in Organizations*. London and New York, NY: Routledge.

34. Dooley, K., T. Johnson, and D. Bush. 1995. "TQM, Chaos, and Complexity." *Human Systems Management* 14, pp. 1–16. https://doi.org/10.3233/HSM-1995-14403.

35. Zaretzky, A.N. 2008. "Quality Management Systems From the Perspective of Organization of Complex Systems." *Mathematical and Computer Modelling* 48, no. 7–8, pp. 1170–1177. ISSN 0895-7177. https://doi.org/10.1016/j.mcm.2007.12.023.

36. Kelly, K. 1994. *Out of Control—The New Biology of Machines, Social Systems, and the Economic World*. Addison-Wesley Publishing Company.

37. Syed, M. 2021. *Rebel Ideas*. John Murray.

38. Jeffrey, A.F., A. Leibbrandt, C. Rott, and O. Stoddard. 2021. "Increasing Workplace Diversity: Evidence From a Recruiting Experiment at a Fortune 500 Company." *Journal of Human Resources* 56, no. 1, pp. 73–92. University of Wisconsin Press. https://doi.org/10.3368/jhr.56.1.0518-9489R1.

39. Greenleaf, R.K. 2002. *Servant Leadership: A Journey Into the Nature of Legitimate Power and Greatness*. Paulist Press.

40. Sorgvist, L. 2014. "Future Development of the Quality Profession." International Conference on Quality—Toyko 14 Published at ICQ'14-Tokyo. http://h24-files.s3.amazonaws.com/229042/793773-vU3Qm.pdf.

41. Alvesson, M. and A. Spicer. 2016. *The Stupidity Paradox*. London: Profile Books Ltd.

42. Sweet, S. and P. Meiksins. 2008. *Changing Contours of Work: Job and Opportunities in the New Economy*. Thousand Oaks: Pine Forge Press.

43. Sweet, S. and P. Meiksins. 2020. *Changing Contours of Work: Job and Opportunities in the New Economy*, ed. 4. Sage Publications.

44. National Academy of Science and Engineering. 2013. "Recommendations for Implementing the Strategic Initiative INDUSTRIE 4.0. Final Report of the Industry 4.0 Working Group." din.de. www.din.de/blob/76902/e8cac883f42bf28536e7e8165993f1fd/recommendations-for-implementing-industry-4-0-data.pdf.

45. Johnson, S. February 2019. "Quality 4.0: A Trend Within a Trend." *Quality* 58, no. 2, pp. 21–23. www.qualitymag.com/articles/95272-quality-40-a-trend-within-a-trend.

46. Watson, G.H. 2019. "The Ascent of Quality 4.0." *Quality Progress* 52, no. 3, pp. 24–30. asq.org. https://asq.org/quality-progress/articles/the-ascent-of-quality-40?id=8321f828c7c44634b996b2b1ba25a315.

47. Lyle, M.A. 2017. "From Paper and Pencil to Industry 4.0: Revealing the Value of Data Through Quality Intelligence." *Quality Magazine* 56, pp. 25–29. qualitymag.com. www.qualitymag.com/articles/94259-from-paper-and-pencil-to-industry-40-revealing-the-value-of-data-through-quality-intelligence.

48. MedTech Europe. 2021. *Facts and Figures*. www.medtecheurope.org/wp-content/uploads/2021/06/medtech-europe-facts-and-figures-2021.pdf.

49. Jackall, R. 2010. *Moral Mazes: The World of Corporate Managers*. New York, NY: Oxford University Press.

50. Collins, J. 2001. *Good To Great: Why Some Companies Make the Leap... and Others Don't*. London: Random House Business Books.

51. Radziwill, N.M. 2018. "Quality 4.0: Let's Get Digital—The Many Ways the Fourth Industrial Revolution Is Reshaping the Way We Think About Quality." ArXiv abs/1810.07829.

52. Anders, F., J. Lilja, Y. Lagrosen, and B. Bergquist. 2020. "Quality 2030: Quality Management for the Future." *Total Quality Management & Business Excellence*. https://doi.org/10.1080/14783363.2020.1863778.

53. International Standards Organization. June 2022. "ISO14001:2015, Environmental management Systems—Requirements With Guidance for Use." iso.org. www.iso.org/standard/60857.html.

54. Bushe, G.R. and Marshak, R.J. 2015. "Dialogic Organization Development: The Theory and Practice of Transformational Change." Berrett-Koehler Publishers, Inc.

55. Forbes Insights. 2014. *Culture of Quality: Accelerating Growth and Performance Within the Enterprise*. New York, NY: 60 Fifth avenue. https://images.forbes .com/forbesinsights/StudyPDFs/ASQ_CultureofQuality_REPORT.pdf.

56. Srinivasan, A. and B. Kurey. April 2014. "Organizational Culture: Creating a Culture of Quality." *Harvard Business Review*. hbr.org.

57. Hunt, J. 2022. *Zero: Eliminating Unnecessary Deaths in a Post-Pandemic*. London: NHS Swift Press.

58. Czaja, R. and J. Blair. 2005. *Designing Surveys—A Guide to Decisions and Procedures*, 2nd ed. Thousand Oaks, London; New Delhi: Pine Forge Press. Sage Publications, Inc.

About the Authors

Matthew P. Wictome, PhD, is Managing Director and founder of Datod Consulting. Datod specializes in building better and more effective Quality organizations. Over the past 30 years, he has worked closely with a wide range of companies implementing impactful change to better serve the customer, benefit the shareholder, and improve regulatory compliance. Apart from holding qualifications in lean and Six Sigma, he is an ISO13485 quality system lead auditor. He holds a PhD and graduate degree in Biochemistry and an executive masters in Strategy, Change, and Leadership with the University of Bristol. He is passionate in designing and implementing quality systems that are effective, efficient, and outcome driven. His interests include how organizations function in the real world and the role of organizational culture has on the management of quality.

Ian Wells, PhD, is Vice President of Quality Assurance and Regulatory Affairs for Trinity Biotech. Over the past 30 years, he has worked in R&D, Operations and Quality/Regulatory, for a range of companies in the Pharmaceutical and Medical Device fields. His focus has been on the implementation of small and large change programs to drive the removal of nonvalue adding processes from quality systems and provide enhanced customer outcomes. He holds a PhD and graduate degree in analytical chemistry and chemometrics. Ian is passionate about finding and developing the best talent, is a trained coach, and has spent a large proportion of his professional life working in a variety of countries and cultures. Through experience, he has developed a methodology of strategic quality change based on the concept of the T-map and its use to bring out the best in people and process and the technology used to support them.

Index

Concise and Applied Business Books

The Collection listed above is one of 30 business subject collections that Business Expert Press has grown to make BEP a premiere publisher of print and digital books. Our concise and applied books are for…

- Professionals and Practitioners
- Faculty who adopt our books for courses
- Librarians who know that BEP's Digital Libraries are a unique way to offer students ebooks to download, not restricted with any digital rights management
- Executive Training Course Leaders
- Business Seminar Organizers

Business Expert Press books are for anyone who needs to dig deeper on business ideas, goals, and solutions to everyday problems. Whether one print book, one ebook, or buying a digital library of 110 ebooks, we remain the affordable and smart way to be business smart. For more information, please visit www.businessexpertpress.com, or contact sales@businessexpertpress.com.

www.ingramcontent.com/pod-product-compliance
Lightning Source LLC
Chambersburg PA
CBHW061313220326
41599CB00026B/4860